Order Flow Analyses and Foreign Exchange Dealing

T0316431

STUDIEN ZU INTERNATIONALEN WIRTSCHAFTSBEZIEHUNGEN

Herausgegeben von Prof. Dr. Michael Frenkel

Band 4

PETER LANG

Frankfurt am Main · Berlin · Bern · Bruxelles · New York · Oxford · Wien

Alexander Mende

Order Flow Analyses and Foreign Exchange Dealing

PETER LANG

Europäischer Verlag der Wissenschaften

Bibliographic Information published by Die Deutsche Bibliothek
Die Deutsche Bibliothek lists this publication in the Deutsche Nationalbibliografie; detailed bibliographic data is available in the internet at <http://dnb.ddb.de>.

Zugl.: Hannover, Univ., Diss., 2004

D 89
ISSN 1618-503X
ISBN 3-631-53571-6
US-ISBN 0-8204-7689-7

© Peter Lang GmbH
Europäischer Verlag der Wissenschaften
Frankfurt am Main 2005
All rights reserved.

Printed in Germany 1 2 4 5 6 7

www.peterlang.de

Table of Contents

1 An Introduction to the Order Flow Analysis of Foreign Exchange Trading

1.1 Motivation   7

1.2 The microstructure approach to exchange rates   10

    1.2.1 Private information, order flow and bid-ask spreads   10

    1.2.2 Trading on the foreign exchange market   13

1.3 Empirical studies on foreign exchange market microstructure   15

1.4 Outline   17

2 Asymmetric Information and Foreign Exchange Dealing

2.1 Introduction   19

2.2 Data   21

2.3 Small banks and large banks   27

    2.3.1 Baseline spreads   30

    2.3.2 Influence of asymmetric information or prospective inventories   30

    2.3.3 Influence of existing inventory   31

    2.3.4 Inventory management   32

2.4 Spread variation across customers and trade size   36

    2.4.1 Financial and corporate customers   36

    2.4.2 Trade size   39

    2.4.3 Information in currency markets   43

2.5 The asymmetric information share of currency spreads   48

2.6 Conclusions   50

3 Profit Sources in FX Trading

3.1 Introduction   59

3.2 Data   60

3.3 Overall revenue and profit   62

3.4 Revenues from the trader's speculation   65

    3.4.1 Approaches identifying revenues from speculation   65

    3.4.2 Revenues from accumulating inventory?   67

    3.4.3 Revenues beyond customer trading?   71

    3.4.4 Revenues due to price volatility?   73

    3.4.5 Correlates of daily revenues   74

3.5 Profits from different sources   77

    3.5.1 Profits from speculation, interbank and customer trading   77

    3.5.2 Profits from financial and commercial customers   78

    3.5.3 Profits from small, medium and large customers   79

3.6 Conclusions   81

4 September 11th on the Foreign Exchange Market

4.1 Introduction	85
4.2 Data description	86
4.3 Foreign exchange trading during the events of September 11th	93
4.3.1 Trading volume, volatility and spreads in the literature	93
4.3.2 Impact and persistence of September 11th on daily trading determinants	95
4.3.3 Having a closer look at the high-frequency data	107
4.4 Conclusion	112

5 Tobin Tax Effects Seen from the Foreign Exchange Market's Microstructure

5.1 Introduction	115
5.2 The Tobin tax concept	117
5.3 Confronting the Tobin tax hypotheses with recent market microstructure findings	120
5.3.1 Do banks dominate the market through short-term speculation?	120
5.3.2 Do short-term horizons indicate non-fundamentalism?	124
5.3.3 Does a Tobin tax reduce excessive exchange rate volatility?	125
5.3.4 Can any tax rate satisfy the guidance and the liquidity objective?	128
5.4 Policy conclusions	129

References — 131

1 An Introduction to the Order Flow Analysis of Foreign Exchange Trading[*]

1.1 Motivation

Ever since the work of Meese and Rogoff (1983), traditional exchange rate modeling has been in crisis. In their classic paper, Meese and Rogoff show that a simple random walk describes the movement of exchange rates better than approaches relying on any given set of macroeconomic variables. The number of studies confirming the poor empirical power of such fundamental asset approaches is huge (for surveys see Frankel and Rose, 1995; or Taylor, 1995). The bottom line is that fundamentals cannot explain exchange rates.[1] Therefore, models using solely macro variables are bound to fail empirically, since they do not capture what is actually happening on foreign exchange markets. However, it is commonly believed that fundamental approaches are not wrong altogether (Lyons, 2001a, p.3), but rather missing some important features that matter for exchange rates.[2] The question about the "inner life" of foreign exchange markets arises. How do these markets really work and (how) does the trading process eventually influence exchange rates? Questions about the "microstructure of foreign exchange markets" come to the fore. Which aspects of foreign exchange trading have an impact on prices, and which do not? These problems might always have been of interest to practitioners, but now they are becoming particularly important from a theoretical point of view.

Since the middle of the 1990s, there is now an empirically motivated approach to exchange rates in this spirit, based on the analysis of order flows. Foreign exchange market microstructure addresses the actual trading process and corresponding aspects of foreign exchange trading, i.e. the flow of orders and the structure of the foreign exchange market with its players. The future aim is to establish "new micro exchange rate economics" by incorporating the order flow component into the modeling process (Lyons, 2001a). Analyses of order

---

* For helpful comments I would like to thank Lukas Menkhoff, Torben Lütje, Michael Frömmel and Josefin Cejie.

1 As a consequence, for the past 20 years there have been numerous attempts to overcome these staggering results. But, while pure statistical approaches do a great job in reproducing stylized facts about foreign exchange rates, they lack an economic background. Approaches from the wide field of behavioral finance have been enlightening theoretically, but proved to be comparatively less successful empirically. E.g., rational bubbles theory, herding behavior, noise trading and similar approaches either focus on a single aspect of foreign exchange trading, or their empirical results hold for a certain period of time only.

2 In fact, a lot of people in the foreign exchange practice do consider such models as generally appropriate and make use of them. For example, in a study conducted by Gehrig and Menkhoff (2004) 32.4% of foreign exchange dealers consider themselves as "fundamentalists".

flows have become a promising field of research as cumulated flows are closely related to exchange rate movements (see Lyons, 2001a; Killeen, Lyons and Moore, 2001; Evans and Lyons, 2002, 2003; Fan and Lyons, 2003; Mende, Menkhoff and Osler, 2004). Figure 1.1 provides a few illustrating examples. This recently uncovered fact about order flows is an additional motivation, beyond successfully applying ideas, methods and tools of the finance literature to foreign exchange markets, to capture the behavior of foreign exchange dealers themselves (Madhavan, 2000).

The pioneering research of foreign exchange market order flow analyses was conducted by Lyons (1995), who examined the trading behavior of a large US dealer over one week in 1992. This study was the first of its kinds to show the importance of order flow for the decision-making of foreign exchange dealers and, thus, defining a new kind of "order flow information". It has triggered a number of successive studies – like this dissertation – which further extend the insights of this relatively new approach.[3]

This dissertation is made up of four related studies in the spirit of this new microstructure approach to exchange rates. It contributes to the existing literature by extending our knowledge of microstructure effects in the decision-making of foreign exchange dealers: Chapter 2 provides evidence that dealers behave strategically to increase the information content of their incoming order flow. While foreign currency prices are mainly driven by bigger, informed players, profits at a (small) foreign exchange dealing bank are largely generated by engaging in business with less informed market participants (see Chapter 3). To broaden our view, we also take a look at the interplay of the overall foreign exchange market determinants and trading activity at times of market stress (Chapter 4). Founded by our microstructure insights, we finally offer some policy implications regarding the Tobin tax – which would directly affect trading on the foreign exchange market (Chapter 5). In this manner, we hope to further pave the way for foreign exchange market microstructure research.

This chapter continues with a short introduction to the microstructure approach to exchange rates in Section 1.2. Section 1.3 provides a brief overview of the existing empirical studies in this field of research. In Section 1.4, we outline the following chapters in detail.

---

3   For a regularly updated list of papers on foreign exchange microstructure, please refer to www.microstructure.org.

Figure 1.1 Order flows and exchange rate movements

A Incoming interbank order flow and FX prices (tick-by-tick)

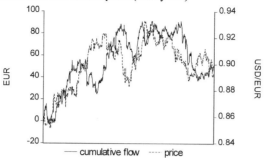

Source: Mende, Menkhoff and Osler (2004)

B Cumulative customer order flow and exchange rates (months)

Source: Fan and Lyons (2003)

C Four months of exchange rates (solid) and order flow (dashed), May 1 – August 31, 1996 (daily)

DM/$ ¥/$

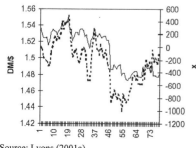
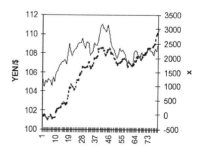

Source: Lyons (2001a)

9

1.2 The microstructure approach to exchange rates

1.2.1 Private information, order flow and bid-ask spreads

To understand the basic principles of the microstructure approach it is necessary to explain its three main components.[4] (i) Private information exists. Microstructure models assume that there is some information relevant to exchange rates, which is not publicly available. (ii) Two variables – taken from the finance literature – which are irrelevant in traditional macroeconomic models play a major role in this context, i.e. bid-ask spreads and order flow. (iii) The distinct structure of the foreign exchange market, i.e. different players and institutional setups, needs to be incorporated in the process of modeling because it influences the decision-making of market participants and eventually the formation of prices.

"Information is private if it is not known by all people and if it produces a better price forecast than public information alone." (Lyons, 2001a, pp.26) The interpretation of news for instance can be regarded as private information. News about macroeconomic variables is published regularly and is available to all market participants at the same time. Thus, news is public information. However, the way a single market participant evaluates this news and what kind of decision follows remains hidden to the public. The resulting trading behavior itself is then informative. This private information affects foreign exchange prices, too. Several empirical studies have confirmed the existence of private information and its – at least short-term – influence on market prices for different foreign exchange markets (see Ito, Lyons and Melvin, 1998; and Rime, 2000). Within the trading process order flow contains such private information. It serves as a vehicle for information into prices. The interaction of order flow, private and public information is illustrated in Figure 1.2.

Figure 1.2 The role of order flow

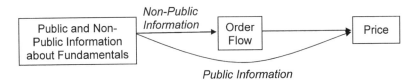

Source: Lyons (2001a, Figure 7.1, p.175)

---

4   Lyons (2001a) provides a broad and detailed overview.

Order flow is signed trading volume. If a trade is buyer (seller) initiated a "+" ("−") is attached to the original transaction.[5] In addition to fundamental and technical analyses of foreign exchange markets, analyses based on order flows have become more and more important to dealers within the last years (see Gehrig and Menkhoff, 2004). Private information can either be incorporated in each single transaction or it can be detected due to the inventory position of a dealer. Knowing about their own customer order flow, dealers (temporarily) benefit from the information advantage they gain towards other less informed dealers. Thus, they do not only act as intermediates for their customers, but actually profit by the information contained in these orders (Cao, Evans and Lyons, 2004). It helps them to position themselves and get a better view of what is happening on the market. The larger one's client-ship the better informed a dealer is considered to be. Besides those customer orders, so-called incoming interbank trades are regarded as informative too, as other dealers might have access to their very own customer base as well. Thus, dealers recognize that they might experience losses if they trade with a better informed counterparty. Unfortunately they cannot identify those better informed dealers a priori. These information asymmetries produce an adverse selection problem. Dealers protect themselves against the costs of adverse selection by adjusting their bid-ask spread to the trade size and to the assumed informativeness of the opponent by setting larger spreads for larger orders.[6]

Customer orders and transactions of other dealers do not only contain private information. They affect the inventory position of dealers directly. Thus, order flow also shows if a dealer is *short* or *long* at the time of the transaction. In this context the term "hot potato trading" has been introduced to the microstructure literature (Lyons, 1996, 1997; see also Mende, 2002). Hot potato trading is the passing-on of open inventory positions between dealers in the course of sharing price risks "collectively".[7] Information asymmetries increase transaction costs and hamper the search for counterparties. A dealer who wants to pass on a "hot potato" might have to break it down into smaller orders, in order to avoid disadvantages during the price setting. Thus, numerous market participants have to rebalance their inventory positions. Hence, the process of risk sharing becomes broader and more important for what is happening on the market. These

---

5   In multiple dealer markets (direct interbank trades) the quoting market maker takes the non-initiating side. In an auction market (indirect brokered interbank trades) limit orders are considered as non-initiating. When it comes to customer-dealer-trades customers always take the initiating side.
6   In this connection, the heterogeneity of market participants plays a distinctive role. Please see next section for further details.
7   Foreign exchange dealers themselves believe that such hot potato trading causes the huge turnover figures on the interbank market (see Lyons, 2001b, p.7).

"natural" variations of inventory positions have an impact on the exchange rate itself and might cause temporary misallocations (Flood, 1994, p.149).

In dealer markets bid-ask spreads typically reflect three types of costs: first, order processing costs occur in the course of executing an order. Second, inventory costs are associated with the costs of holding open positions due to being exposed to exchange rate risk. Third, as aforementioned, asymmetric information costs arise to account for the possibility that the counterpart is privately informed. Whereas the first cost component should be independent from the actual size of an order, inventory costs and asymmetric information costs are expected to be positively correlated with order size as the corresponding risks increase (see Figure 1.3). The common theoretical background from the market microstructure literature is the by-now canonical model of currency dealer pricing, which was originally developed in Lyons (1995) as an extension of the model in Madhavan and Smidt (1991) which, in turn, is based on Kyle's (1985) asymmetric information model for equity markets. It postulates that pricing decisions captured in the setting of bid-ask spreads will be influenced, among other things, by the cost-effects mentioned above: firstly, an asset's own inventory will influence price setting by promoting deals, leading to a mean-reversion of the inventory, i.e. the inventory effect. Secondly, dealers acknowledge asymmetric information among market participants in the sense that they assume private information when they set prices for a larger potential deal, i.e. the information effect. Finally, traders live from buying low and selling high, so a baseline spread is to be expected. The examination of these three effects is at the core of most foreign exchange market microstructure studies.

Figure 1.3 The components of the bid-ask spread

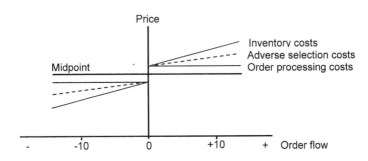

1.2.2 Trading on the foreign exchange market

Microstructure analyses also account for the specific structure of currency markets – including their institutional characteristics. Rime (2003) provides a detailed overview (and outlook) of the recent technical and structural developments on the foreign exchange markets. How can one describe the state of these markets in short?

International foreign exchange markets are quite different compared to other financial markets. First, their decentralized organization and the number of market participants allows for trading foreign currencies worldwide around-the-clock. Second, the huge turnover figures – especially in the spot market – stand out. In 2001 the daily turnover in the spot foreign exchange markets amounted to USD 387 billions on average (BIS, 2002, p.5). Compared to other financial markets, the share of interdealer business in the foreign exchange market is also striking. Although this share has decreased from 64% in 1998 to 59% in 2001, approximately USD 589 billions are still transacted just between dealers every day (cf. BIS, 1999 and 2002). Aside from its multiple dealer structure, foreign exchange markets are characterized by a high degree of concentration, e.g. in Germany 75% of all foreign exchange turnover is conducted by only five banks compared to 33 participating banks (see BIS, 2002, p.10).[8] So, there are a few big players and many small – sometimes marginal – ones.

Heterogeneity of market participants and the various ways of transacting deals define the structure of the foreign exchange market beyond those raw figures. There is a strict segmentation of the market into interdealer-trades on the one hand and customer-dealer-trades on the other. Within interbank trading, microstructure literature differentiates between market makers, jobbers and intermediates. Market makers are dealers who quote buy and sell prices upon request. They provide liquidity services (immediacy) to the market. A market maker receives compensation through the quoted spread.[9] Jobbers make profits by buying and selling smaller positions rapidly without any customer business in the background (see Lyons, 1998). Intermediates rather just square their customer orders at the interbank market than trading for their own account. However, they realize significant profits by quoting larger spreads within the customer business (see Mende and Menkhoff, 2004). The underlying motivation for trading and profit-making of dealers as well as their individual degree of informativeness – due to business size and customer base – determines the decision-making and the quoted spreads between dealers.

When it comes to customer-dealer-trades, order size does matter for customer business (Mende, Menkhoff and Osler, 2004). So does the informative-

---

8   In the US 13 of 79 participating trading offices take on 75% of foreign exchange trading volume, in the UK 17 of 257 (see BIS, 2002, p.10).
9   There is no formal obligation to quote tight spreads though. Instead, market making is governed by reciprocity (see Rime, 2003).

ness and the underlying motivation for dealing in foreign currencies. Institutional investors for instance, i.e. large financial institutions such as insurance companies or pension funds, are considered to be better informed than "regular" non-financial corporations. Their order flow has considerable influence on the decision-making of foreign exchange dealers (Carpenter and Wang, 2003), they are quoted better spreads (Mende, Menkhoff and Osler, 2004) and thus, they affect prices and exchange rates (Fan and Lyons, 2003; Mende, Menkhoff and Osler, 2004).

Dealers are networked worldwide 24 hours a day. They provide liquidity to each other and regularly exchange information.[10] Customers can only operate currency transactions with one or more banks directly by requesting prices from the bank's sales staff. At the interbank market trades can either be transacted directly between two dealers or indirectly via brokers. When choosing brokered trades a dealer stays anonymous. During the last decade electronic brokering systems, such as Electronic Brokering Services (EBS) and Reuters Dealing D2000-2, have increasingly replaced traditional voice brokers and direct trading channels. This has led to a substantial change in trading behavior (see Bjønnes and Rime, 2003; Rime, 2003; Carpenter and Wang, 2003). It has also increased the transparency of foreign exchange markets as market-wide order flow can now be observed on the dealers' screens. However, because of the anonymity of market participants and the discrimination of customer orders, the transparency of foreign exchange markets is still low compared to other financial markets (see Lyons, 2001a, p.41).[11]

Figure 1.4 shows the structure of the foreign exchange market and its trading channels in a simplified way. Central banks play a key role on the foreign exchange market. They are regarded as especially well-informed and influential in the short run (see Carpenter and Wang, 2003). By intervening often – openly as well as hidden – they are among the big players in this market. However, in microstructure literature their influence on exchange rates in the long run is controversial (see Vitale, 1999; and Galati, 2003).

These structural characteristics (heterogeneity of market participants and institutional setting) on the one hand and the microstructure effects due to private information mentioned above on the other, do significantly effect the price formation on the foreign exchange markets from a "microstructure researcher's" point of view.

---

10 Dealers have told us that they actually phone each other to talk about the latest market developments or even a single extraordinary large order passing through the market.

11 A few years back, some major banks offered their larger customers direct access to interdealer foreign exchange markets by implementing dealer-platforms on the internet, such as FXall or Atriax. This experiment failed because liquidity stayed very low and banks did not make enough profits to run these platforms (see Rime, 2003).

Figure 1.4 Participants and trading channels in foreign exchange trading

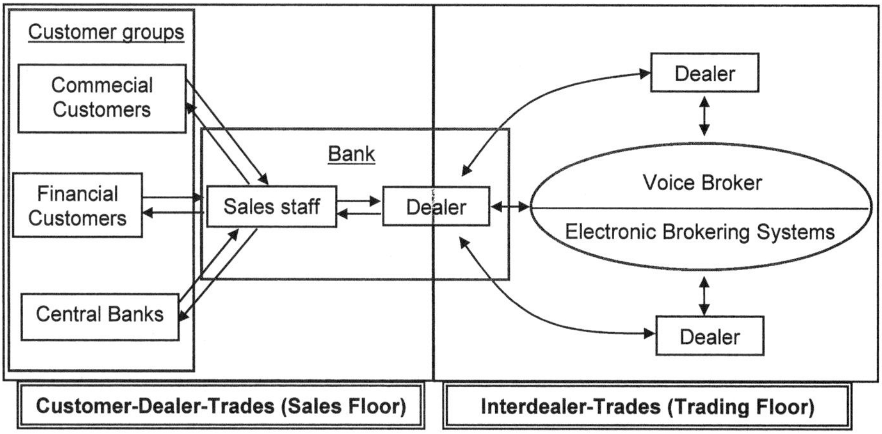

Customer groups

| Commecial Customers |
| Financial Customers |
| Central Banks |

Bank — Sales staff — Dealer

Dealer

Voice Broker
Electronic Brokering Systems

Dealer

Customer-Dealer-Trades (Sales Floor)   Interdealer-Trades (Trading Floor)

1.3 Empirical studies on foreign exchange market microstructure

Unfortunately, empirical foreign exchange microstructure research is still in the fledgling stages due to a lack of adequate data available, i.e. actual transaction data of a foreign exchange dealing bank (so-called tick-by-tick data) (Lyons 2001a, pp.114-126).

Many event-studies show the usefulness of order flow analyses. Ito, Lyons and Melvin (1998), Rime (2000), and Covrig and Melvin (2002) find evidence for the existence of private information in foreign exchange markets. Surveys reveal the importance of order flow analyses to dealers themselves (see Cheung, Chinn and March, 2000; Cheung and Chinn, 2001; Gehrig and Menkhoff, 2004). Recent studies aim to explain exchange rate movements directly by order flow information. Hau, Killeen and Moore (2000), Killeen, Lyons and Moore (2001), Evans and Lyons (2002, 2003), Evans (2002), and Froot and Ramadorai (2002) show that cumulated order flows and exchange rates are positively correlated for different time horizons.

Whereas these studies highlight the general power of order flow analyses, studies which directly focus on the decision-making of foreign exchange market participants, in particular dealers, are scarce. Order flow itself is a variable that needs to be explained. Thus, it is essential to study the trading behavior of dealers if you want to understand foreign exchange markets. The necessary data belongs to banks though. It is of proprietary nature and therefore difficult to obtain.[12]

We contribute to the literature by introducing yet another data set, the fourth of its kind. According to our knowledge only three other comparable data sets have been studied before, i.e. Lyons (1995), Yao (1998a), and Bjønnes and Rime (2003).[13] Differences of the underlying data sets should be mentioned briefly.[14] Lyons (1995) analyzes one large USD/DEM dealer for a week in August 1992. His dealer does not have any customer business at all and can be characterized as a jobber. Yao (1998a) is focusing on a large USD/DEM market maker in 1995. His data set covers 25 trading days altogether. Unlike Lyons' dealer, this dealer has a remarkable share of customer business of roughly 14%. Bjønnes and Rime (2003) are studying the foreign exchange trading of four different dealers at a medium-sized Norwegian bank for a week in 1998.[15]

We have managed to collect the longest observation period of foreign exchange trading existing of actual tick-by-tick data. Our data set covers the total trading activity of a small bank in Germany for 87 trading days in 2001. The fact that we study the decision-making at a small dealing bank now enables us to look at the whole range of dealer types. Besides, we analyze the largest customer share in foreign exchange microstructure research up to date and, for the first time, make intensive use of disaggregating order flows into different counterparties, i.e. interbank, financial and commercial customer business, and accounting for trade size categories at the same time. For a more detailed description of our data set please see Chapters 2 and 3. The analysis of this data set brings out interesting similarities with other studies, as well as contrasting results complementing and differentiating our knowledge about the microstructure of foreign exchange dealing.

---

12 Related studies often use so-called Reuters FXFX "Indicative Quotes" instead (see Goodhart, 1988; Goodhart and Figliuoli; 1991; Bollerslev and Domowitz, 1993; Peiers, 1997; Danielsson and Payne, 2001; and Dominguez, 2003; among others), which are publicly available. Though, a lot of important aspects of microstructure research, such as bid-ask spreads and volatility issues, can be analyzed by quoted data, they do not allow for observing actual trading behavior and real order flow (Lyons, 2001a, pp.124-125).

13 Carpenter and Wang (2003) use a data set that stems from 2002, while our data set was obtained in 2001. Related issues are studied in Lyons (1998), Yao (1998b), Bjønnes and Rime (2001), and Romeu (2003). These studies each use the same data set though.

14 For detailed descriptions of the data sets please refer to the original literature.

15 Carpenter and Wang (2003) analyze a similar Australian bank for a period of 45 trading days in 2002.

1.4 Outline

The remainder of this dissertation is organized as follows. In Chapter 2 we examine how asymmetric information affects quotes at a foreign exchange dealing bank. We show that spreads are narrowest when counterparties are most likely to be informed. Specifically, spreads are narrowest for relatively large deals with financial customers and with other market makers. This practice is not predicted by models of non-strategic dealing under asymmetric information. We hypothesize, that currency dealers set spreads strategically, subsidizing informative deal flow in order to benefit from the information. Models of non-strategic dealing prove helpful, nonetheless, because the "asymmetric information" share of spreads is generally highest when counterparties are most likely to be informed. We hypothesize that the "information" sought by currency dealers could either concern exchange rate fundamentals or transient aspects of trading, and provide arguments to favor the latter. Our data comprise the complete deal record of USD/EUR trades at a small bank in Germany during four months of 2001, with customer trades disaggregated into financial and commercial customers.

The study we present in Chapter 3 identifies and examines the profits made in the USD/EUR-trading of the same bank. We find that speculative positions fail to become profitable within a 30-minutes' horizon. A spread analysis reveals that there is no room for revenues from speculation. Also, the suggestion that exchange rate volatility would foster speculative profits cannot be confirmed. Finally, it is only customer business that emerges as a significant profit source in a multivariate approach. Disaggregated analyses reveal that commercial customers are more profitable than financial customers. The most profit is generated by large commercial customer orders.

Chapter 4 provides a more general view of the foreign exchange market. On September 11th 2001 terrorists crashed hijacked airliners into the two towers of the World Trade Center and the Pentagon. We study the relationship between foreign exchange trading activities, volatility and bid-ask spreads on the USD/EUR foreign exchange market on the basis of an extended data set. We find that volatility and spreads are by far larger during the events of September 11th, but the shock is not persistent. The positive correlation between volume, volatility and spreads does not break up, but intensifies strongly indicating the arrival of new information and increased price risk. The foreign exchange market maintains its liquid structure and its efficient processing of exogenous shocks.

Finally, in Chapter 5 we provide some policy implications. The Tobin tax is in high demand by many groups. Despite its popularity, research has not yet made full use of available insights from the microstructure literature. The role of banks in foreign exchange trading is quite different from what proponents usually assume. The most probable decisive group for shorter-term exchange rate movements is asset managers. They speculate under comparatively longer hori-zons than foreign exchange dealers although they also tend to behave on short-terms. There is no tax rate that could influence their behavior and at the same time keep the desired high liquidity. Thus, no uniform proportional Tobin tax can reach its goals.

2   Asymmetric Information and Foreign Exchange Dealing[*]

2.1   Introduction

Many of the classic papers about market making under asymmetric information, such as Copeland and Galai (1983), Glosten and Milgrom (1985), and Easley and O'Hara (1987), indicate that spreads should widen with the likelihood that a counterparty is informed. This perceived likelihood can be based on the average ratio of informed to uninformed traders (Copeland and Galai, 1983), on trade size (Easley and O'Hara, 1987), or, in some markets, on the identity of the counterparty. Customer identities are known in currency markets, and "financial customers" and other dealers are considered relatively "informed". Thus, these theories, taken together, would imply that spreads in currency markets should be widest for large deals with financial customers and other dealing banks.

This paper shows that spreads in currency markets are *narrowest* for (relatively) large trades with financial customers and banks. We suggest that this reflects attempts by market makers to encourage informed deal flow, by subsidizing the trades most likely to provide useful information.[16] Though not predicted by models of non-strategic dealing under asymmetric information, this result is consistent with the general idea that dealers may shade quotes strategically to increase the share of informative trades. This idea has been explored, in the context of equity trading, in Gammill (1989) and Leach and Madhavan (1992, 1993).

Though currency spreads tend to be highest for the smallest trades with the least "informed" counterparties, contrary to the implications of models of non-strategic dealing, those models still prove relevant. As those models predict, the share of the asymmetric information component of spreads is lowest when counterparties are least likely to be informed.

Our data comprise the entire deal record of a relatively small bank in Germany in USD/EUR over a four-month period in 2001. A major advantage of our dataset is its distinction between financial and commercial customer trades.

---

*   I would like to thank my co-authors Lukas Menkhoff (University of Hannover, Germany) and Carol Osler (Brandeis International Business School, Brandeis University, USA). We are grateful for helpful comments from Alain Chaboud, Thomas Gehrig, Dagfinn Rime, Erik Sirri, Erik Theissen, and Peter Tordo, along with participants at several seminars and the Stockholm Workshop on FOREX Microstructure and International Macroeconomics. We are deeply indebted to the bankers who provided and discussed the data with us. The paper emerged out of an earlier version circulating under the title "Different Counterparties, Different Foreign Exchange Trading? The Perspective of a Median Bank".
16   Indeed, it has long been common knowledge among market participants that currency dealers subsidize "informed" deal flow.

Most existing research focuses exclusively on interbank trades, or considers all customer trades as one category. We find that financial customers are treated quite differently from either corporate customers or other dealing banks. For their large trades they pay virtually no spread, even less than other dealers; for their medium-sized and small trades their spreads are wider than those paid by other dealers but substantially narrower than those paid by corporate customers.

We provide a number of strong reasons why our results will generalize to the currency market as a whole, even though they apply to a small bank. First, insiders at large banks have told us that their pricing policies are the same as those described here. Indeed, the tendency for larger customers to get better treatment in this market is widely known. Hau, Killeen and Moore (2002) remark, for example, "Larger customers may achieve more favorable prices than those provided by the Reuters quotes" (p.158).

Second, we note that the isomorphism between pricing behavior at large and small banks makes economic sense, given the competition in major currency markets. Hundreds of banks deal in the major currency pairs; the largest dealer's market share (that of CITIBANK) is only about 10%. Since competition forces banks to follow the dominant pricing practices, any individual bank's pricing practices should be representative of pricing practices market-wide.

The last reason that our results will generalize to the overall market is that, in other important ways, our small bank behaves just like large banks. We document that our small dealer's spreads on interbank trades match those estimated for large banks (Lyons, 1995; Hau, Killeen and Moore, 2002; Bjønnes and Rime, 2003). Likewise, our small dealer keeps his inventory quite close to zero, like dealers at large banks (Bjønnes and Rime, 2003). Finally, our small dealer's quoted spreads are not affected by his inventory level, and he tends to manage his inventory through outgoing interbank deals; these behaviors, too, are shared with dealers at large banks (Bjønnes and Rime, 2003; Yao, 1998a). Thus, a second contribution of the paper is to show that pricing practices are consistent across all sizes of dealing banks.

Our central hypothesis, that currency dealers subsidize informed deal flow, raises an important question: What kind of "information" are they hoping to gather? There are basically two possibilities. First, they could be hoping to gather information about exchange rate fundamentals. We provide evidence that this bank's interbank and financial customer order flows are both positively cointegrated with exchange rates, consistent with the hypothesis that these components of order flow provide such fundamental information.

Two observations suggest, however, that banks may not be seeking fundamental information. First, "fundamentals" are primarily relevant in the long run, but currency dealers generally close their positions by the end of the day. Second, the kind of inside information about fundamentals relevant to equity markets (How capable is management? What is the big competitor's next product?) seems likely to be fairly scarce in currency markets. The "fundamental" determinants of exchange rates – generally viewed as broad macroeconomic aggregates such as money supplies, price levels, and average risk aversion – are either public information or not measured at all.

Thus, it is plausible that the information currency dealers seek concerns transient aspects of trading, rather than fundamentals. In particular, we note that currency deal flow is correlated – there tend to be "runs" of buy orders and "runs" of sell orders (Goodhart, Ito and Payne, 1996). We discuss various trading practices that would generate exactly this tendency. When order flow comes in runs, there is a clear incentive to gather information that would indicate the beginning of a run.

The paper proceeds as follows: Section 2.2 describes our data. Section 2.3 shows that our small bank dealer sets prices and manages inventories the same as large bank dealers. This means that the conclusions of the rest of our analysis are likely to generalize to the rest of the currency market. In Section 2.4 we show that our dealer quotes narrower spreads for financial customers than commercial customers, and wider spreads on small customer trades than large ones. It suggests that currency dealers strategically gather information through the trading process, and discuss the nature of the relevant "information". This section concludes with a list of reasons why the relationship between spreads and information could vary between stock and currency markets. Section 2.5 shows that the share of the asymmetric information component of spreads is largest when counterparties are most likely to be informed, consistent with models of non-strategic dealing under asymmetric information. Section 2.6 concludes.

2.2 Data

Our data comprise the complete USD/EUR trading record of a German bank over the 87 trading days from 11 July, 2001 to 9 November, 2001. This is the longest existing observation period for currency dealer transactions. For each trade, we have the following information:
(1) the date and time[17]
(2) the type of counterparty: bank, financial customer, commercial customer
(3) the initiator of the trade
(4) the direction of each trade (bank buys or sells)
(5) the quantity traded
(6) the transaction price
(7) the forward points if applicable

---

17 The time stamp indicates the time of data entry and not the moment of trade execution, which will differ slightly. Nevertheless there is no allocation problem because all trades are entered in a strict chronological order.

We identify whether the transactions price was a bid or offer, and whether the trade was incoming or outgoing, by noting the trade-initiating party. Approximately 53% of all trades are incoming, a figure similar to that of the big bank analyzed in Yao (1998a). Table 2.1 presents statistics about the trades.

Table 2.1   **Comparison of small bank studied here with larger banks studied in other papers**

	This paper	BIS (2002) per bank	Lyons (1995)	Yao (1998a)	Bjønnes and Rime (2003), dealer 2	Carpenter and Wang (2003), AUD/USD dealer
	87 trading days in 2001	April 2001	5 trading days in 1992	25 trading days in 1995	5 trading days in 1998	45 trading days in 2002
Trades per day	40 (51)[a]	---	267	181	198	(58 - 198)[b]	203
Trading value per day (USD mil.)	39 (52)[a]	50 - 150	1,200	1,529	443	(142 - 443)[b]	213
Value per trade (USD mil.)	1.0	---	4.5	8.4	2.2	(1.6 - 4.6)[b]	1.1
Customer share (percent)	23 (39)[a]	33 (world) 25 (Germany)	0	14	3	(0 - 18)[b]	11
Average inventory level, Abs(I_t) (millions)	3.4		11.3	11.0	4.2	(1.30 - 8.57)[b]	---
Average order flow, Abs(Q_t) (millions)	1.2		3.8	9.3	1.8	(1.5 - 3.7)[b]	---
Average price change, Abs(Δp_t) (pips)	11		3	5	5	(5 - 12)[b]	---

[a] Values in parentheses refer to the data set including outright-forward transactions.
[b] Values in parentheses show the range for all 4 dealers.

Daily trading value at our bank was USD 52 million. This is quite small: the BIS finds that average daily foreign exchange trading values range from USD 50 million to USD 150 million per bank. Consistent with this, daily trading values for the large dealers studied elsewhere range from USD 213 million (Carpenter and Wang, 2003) to USD 1,529 million (Yao, 1998a) (Table 2.1). Similarly, our small bank undertook about 51 trades per day, while dealers at the bigger banks studied elsewhere average roughly 200 daily trades.

Though the data technically refer to the overall bank, they are an accurate reflection of a single dealer's behavior because there was only one dealer responsible for the bank's USD/EUR trading. As at large banks, foreign exchange deals at our small bank are split into two segments: (i) trades with other dealers, and (ii) trades with customers. Dealers can contact each other directly or through one of the brokerages. In a direct trade, one bank calls another and asks for a two-way quote for a specific amount. Brokerages take limit orders from dealers and post the best bid and ask prices. Limit orders are then crossed with dealers' market orders.

Dealers at our bank told us that they almost always use EBS, the "Electronic Brokerage System", when possible, for two reasons. First, EBS spreads are very low (one or two "pips" or points); second, communication and transactions require less time on EBS than other trading channels. This preference for dealing through EBS is confirmed by the interbank transactions data. The mean interbank transaction size is EUR 1.42 million (Table 2.2). The standard deviation of interbank trade sizes was also fairly small, at 1.42, and the maximum interbank trade size was only EUR 16 million. The small mean and median interbank transaction size, coupled with the small standard deviation of those sizes, is consistent with existing analyses of electronic brokerages. Hau, Killeen and Moore (2002), for example, find that the mean trade size in USD/EUR was EUR 2 million in 1998-1999. They report personally that almost all such trades were between EUR 1 and EUR 5 million.

Thus, it is not surprising that our average interbank trade size is comparable to recent corresponding figures for larger banks (Bjønnes and Rime, 2003; Carpenter and Wang, 2003). Our average is noticeably smaller than those reported in studies of dealers trading before electronic brokerages came to dominate interbank trading (Lyons, 1995; Yao, 1998a), which is not surprising because average trade sizes are smaller for electronically brokered deals than for direct trades. Further information on the size distribution of trades at our bank is reported in Table 2.3.

Table 2.2   Types of trades

The table shows the complete EUR/USD trading activity of a small German bank over the 87 trading days between July 11th, 2001, and November 9th, 2001.

A   All business

	All trades	Interbank	Customer
All trades			
Number of trades	4,410	1,919	2,491
(percent)	(100)	(44)	(56)
Value of trades (millions)	4,481	2,726	1,755
(percent)	(100)	(61)	(39)
Mean size (millions)	0.98	1.42	0.70
Forward trades			
Number of trades	902	114	788
(percent)	(100)	(13)	(87)
Value of trades (millions)	1,075	87	988
(percent)	(100)	(8)	(92)
Mean size (millions)	1.19	0.76	1.25
Share of all trades (percent)			
By number	20	6	32
By value	24	3	56

B   Customer business

	Total	Financial business	Commercial business	Preferred commercial business
All trades				
Number of trades	2,491	171	1,519	801
(percent)	(100)	(7)	(61)	(32)
Value of trades (millions)	1,755	405	1,204	146
(percent)	(100)	(23)	(69)	(8)
Mean size (millions)	0.70	2.37	0.79	0.18
Forward trades				
Number of trades	788	60	472	256
(percent)	(100)	(8)	(60)	(32)
Value of trades (millions)	988	226	686	76
(percent)	(100)	(23)	(69)	(8)
Mean size (millions)	1.25	3.77	1.45	0.30
Share of all trades (percent)				
By number	32	35	31	32
By value	56	56	57	52

Table 2.3   Size distribution of individual trades, by counterparty

The table shows the size distribution of all EUR-USD spot and forward trades (included in the regressions) at a small German bank over the 87 trading days between July 11th, 2001, and November 9th, 2001.

	Interbank trades	Financial customer trades	Commercial customer trades
Number	1,872	171	1,492
Category	Share (%)		
1 below EUR 0.1 million	7	15	54
2 EUR 0.1 – 0.5 million	9	26	32
3 EUR 0.5 – 1.0 million	7	14	5
4 EUR 1.0 – 20 million	77	44	8
5 EUR 20 million and above	0	1	1

Customers must first speak with a salesperson, requesting a quote for a specific amount.[18] The salesperson relays the request to the interbank dealer specializing in the customer's indicated currency pair. The dealer provides a two-way quote based on market conditions and other relevant information such as recent order flow. The salesperson then decides how much to widen the spread for the customer, if at all. Finally, the customer chooses whether to buy at the salesperson's quoted offer, sell at the salesperson's quoted bid, or decline to deal altogether.

Our ability to distinguish between financial and commercial customers in trade-by-trade data is unique: Lyons (1995) only had data on interbank trading; Yao (1998a) had customer trade data but could not distinguish among customer types; Bjønnes and Rime (2003) did not have enough customer transactions to perform a detailed analysis; and Carpenter and Wang (2003) lacked inventory data to directly test the relevant models; finally, Lyons (2001a) and Fan and Lyons (2003) used data for separated customer groups but on a daily aggregation basis.

Customer trades at our small bank amount to a striking 39 percent of trading volume (23 percent for spot trades only). This does not greatly differ from the 33 percent share of customer trades at all foreign exchange banks (BIS, 2002). It is far larger, however, than the customer shares reported for bigger banks, which range from zero percent (Lyons, 1995) to 14 percent (Yao, 1998a). Customer trading at our bank was dominated by commercial customers, who generated 61 percent of all customer trades and 69 percent of customer trade

---

18   By convention, customers and other banks should also indicate whether the requested amount represents the full amount of their current interest.

value. This dominance of commercial customers at our small bank contrasts with the scene at large banks, as indicated by figures for the whole market: financial customer business is about twice as large as commercial customer business (see BIS, 2002).

The average size of commercial customer trades, EUR 0.79 million, was only one third the average trade size of financial customer trades, EUR 2.37 million (see Table 2.2). This size difference is important, since our evidence shows (and conversations with traders confirm) that trades below EUR 1 million are usually treated less favorably. These customer trade sizes do not differ greatly from those at the large bank considered by Carpenter and Wang (2003), where the average commercial customer trade was USD 0.25 million and the average financial customer trade was USD 1.09 million. They are also consistent with the average USD 3.12 million customer trade size of Bjønnes and Rime (2003).

Outright-forward trades, which account for 20 percent of all trades, were initiated by customers almost 90 percent of the time. We include these trades in our dataset (adjusted to a spot-comparable basis by the forward points) because they account for 32 percent of all customer trades, and 56 percent of all customer trade value. Thus, their inclusion enhances the relevance of our data while simultaneously expanding the dataset. The inclusion of forward trades could theoretically impede direct comparisons between our results and those of earlier papers, which focus exclusively on spot trades. Reassuringly, we find that our results are not qualitatively changed when forward transactions are excluded (results available upon request).

The mean absolute values of order flow at our small bank, $Abs(Q_t)$, was EUR 1.2 million (see Table 2.1; excluding preferred commercial business). This is similar to that of the dealers in Bjønnes and Rime (2003), but smaller than average order flow of USD 3.8 million Lyons' (1995) dealer or the average USD 9.3 million order flow of Yao's (1998a) dealer. The mean absolute change in transaction price between two periods, $Abs(\Delta p_t)$, is 10.7 pips, or roughly 0.001 percent. This is substantially higher than those in closely related studies, presumably because of the relative infrequency of trades at our small bank. It also probably reflects the relatively high proportion of commercial customer trades and of very small trades, for which, as we document below, spreads are highest.

The bank's inventory position is inferred by cumulating successive transactions. As we have no information about a possible overnight position change, we follow Lyons (1995) and set the daily starting position to zero. Figure 2.1 presents this inventory position measured in EUR. Consistent with findings for larger banks (Table 2.1), our small bank keeps its inventory quite low – the average absolute open position during the day is just EUR 3.4 million – and always ends the day with a position close to zero. The similarity between average inventories at small and large banks reflects two offsetting differences noted above: our small bank trades less often, but also trades in smaller volumes.

Figure 2.1 Overall inventory position (in EUR millions)

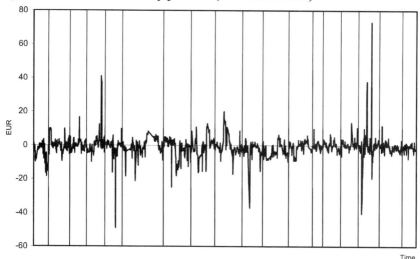

Plot shows the evolution of the dealer's inventory position in EUR millions over the whole sample period (07/11/01 – 11/09/01). The horizontal axis is in transaction-time. Vertical lines indicate the end of each calendar week.

2.3 Small banks and large banks

This section shows that our small bank's pricing and inventory management strategies are generally consistent with those documented for larger banks in the late 1990s.[19] Differences between the small bank's practices and those of larger banks are modest and suggest, consistent with reality, that our small bank has relatively low market power. Those willing to take on faith the similarity between practices at large and small banks can safely skip to the next section, which presents our major results.

The by-now canonical model of currency pricing was originally developed in Lyons (1995) as an extension of the model in Madhavan and Smidt (1991). The model assumes a single dealer considering how to quote, given that his counterparty may have private information about the asset's fundamental value. The model provides a simple linear expression for the price change between incoming transactions:

---

19 Carpenter and Wang (2003) do not document behavior in such detail; in particular the inventory information is missing.

$$\Delta p_t = \alpha + \beta Q_t + \gamma_1 I_t + \gamma_2 I_{t-1} + \delta_1 D_t + \delta_2 D_{t-1} + \eta_t \qquad (1)$$

Here, Δp_t captures the price change in transaction time. Q_t represents the value of the order; I_t and I_{t-1} represent current and lagged inventory; D_t and D_{t-1} represent the current and lagged "direction" of trade – positive (negative) when the counterparty buys (sells) the commodity currency (EUR, for our dealer); η_t represents a random error.

Based on the model, the coefficient on deal size is expected to be positive, reflecting an information effect: larger deals should be more expensive because there is a relatively high likelihood that the counterparty is privately informed (Easley and O'Hara, 1987). It is worth noting, however, that a positive coefficient on order flow could also capture an inventory effect (Ho and Stoll, 1981): larger deals saddle dealers with higher inventory that will likely take longer to work off, bringing greater inventory risk. In this regression setting, the information and inventory motivations are observationally equivalent.

The inventory effect just described, which concerns *prospective* inventories, differs with another inventory effect more familiar in the currency microstructure literature, which concerns *existing* inventories. According to this second effect, the coefficient on current inventory should be negative. If the bank's inventory is large relative to desired inventory, for example, it might quote lower prices to encourage counterparties to buy.[20]

The coefficient on lagged direction should be negative, and its absolute value is theoretically half the baseline spread. In the presence of asymmetric information about fundamentals, the coefficient on current direction should be positive and somewhat larger (in absolute value) than the coefficient on lagged direction.

---

20 A non-zero desired inventory level could be subsumed in the constant term, but most dealers' desired inventory is usually just zero.

Table 2.4   Baseline Lyons/Madhavan-Smidt model

The dependent variable of the below estimation equation is Δp_t, the change in price between two successive trades measured in pips. Q_t is order flow measured in EUR millions multiplied with a dummy variable for each counterparty group, i.e. other dealers, commercial or financial customers respectively. I_t is the dealer's inventory at time t multiplied with a dummy variable for each counterparty group. D_t is an indicator variable picking up the direction of the trade, positive for purchases (at the ask) and negative for sales (at the bid) again multiplied with a dummy variable for each counterparty group. Estimation uses GMM and Newey-West correction. Standard errors in the third column, and "***", "**" and "*" indicate significance at the 1%, 5% and 10%-level respectively.

Panel A $\Delta p_t = \alpha + \beta_1 Q_t + \gamma_1 I_t + \gamma_2 I_{t-1} + \delta_1 D_t + \delta_2 D_{t-1} + \eta_t$

All incoming trades	Coefficient	Standard error
Constant	**-0.599	0.23
Order flow	0.522	0.27
Inventory, Current	*0.503	0.26
Inventory, Lagged	-0.595	0.26
Direction, Current	***7.377	0.39
Direction, Lagged	***-5.347	0.34
Adjusted R^2		0.13
Number of observations		2,859

Panel B $\Delta p_t = \alpha + \beta_1 IBQ_t + \beta_2 CUQ_t + IB(\gamma_1 I_t + \gamma_2 I_{t-1}) + CU(\gamma_3 I_t + \gamma_4 I_{t-1}) + \delta_1 IBD_t + \delta_2 IB(-1)D_{t-1} + \delta_3 CUD_t + \delta_4 CU(-1)D_{t-1} + \eta_t$

All incoming trades	Coefficient	Standard error
Constant	**-0.498	0.22
Order flow		
Interbank	-0.144	0.40
Customer	*0.748	0.42
Inventory		
Interbank trades, Current	-0.253	0.35
Lagged	0.142	0.35
Customer trades, Current	***1.072	0.41
Lagged	***-1.154	0.41
Direction		
Interbank trades, Current	***2.783	0.69
Lagged	***-1.524	0.48
Customer trades, Current	***10.946	0.47
Lagged	***-9.065	0.44
Adjusted R^2		0.23
Number of observations		2,859

The results from this model, applied to all incoming trades, are shown in Table 2.4. To implement these regressions we exclude preferred commercial customer trades, since the associated prices may reflect cross-selling arrangements. We also exclude a few trades with tiny volumes (less than EUR 1,000) or with apparent typographical errors. Price changes are measured in pips; deal and inventory sizes are measured in millions of Euros. Table 2.4, Panel A applies the model to all incoming trades, regardless of counterparty. In Table 2.4, Panel B we distinguish between interdealer trades and trades with customers. In the three sub-sections that follow we discuss baseline spreads and how they are influenced by order quantity and inventory levels. In the final sub-section we examine our dealer's inventory management practices more closely. In all cases we find that our dealer's behavior is largely consistent with dealer behavior at larger banks.21

2.3.1 Baseline spreads

The coefficient on lagged direction, which is theoretically the negative of the baseline half-spread, is about 5.3 pips on average. For interbank trades the average baseline half-spread is only about 1.5 pips, which is consistent with estimates from other studies. Goodhart et al. (2002, p.541), for example, find that the average spread on USD/EUR trades was 2.8 pips over 28 September 1999 to 8 March 2000. The bank appears to distinguish sharply between other dealers and customers, since the average half-spread for customers is 9 pips. A similarly sharp distinction is noted in Bjønnes and Rime (2001a) for the NOK/DEM dealer; for that dealer, as well as our dealer, the ratio of customer spread to dealer spread is 6. This is especially interesting because, though Bjønnes and Rime's NOK/DEM dealer works at a large bank, a high fraction of his order flow comes from customers, similarly to our dealer.

2.3.2 Influence of asymmetric information or prospective inventories

The coefficient on trade size, Q_t, is positive but statistically insignificant in all cases, suggesting that neither information asymmetries nor prospective inventories cause larger deals to be priced less attractively. Though this is not predicted by the Lyons/Madhavan-Smidt model cited above, it is largely consis-

---

21 Note: In order to check the robustness of the results presented below, we repeated the baseline model of Table 2.4 for interbank spot trades only (see Annex 2.1). In addition, the related but more disaggregated model of the later Table 2.7 is presented here (see Annex 2.2), for monthly sub-periods (Annex 2.3) and with OLS regressions where appropriate. We also restricted the data set to transactions within 5, 10, 15, or 20 minutes of each other (see Annex 2.4 for transactions within 15 minutes). These results, further details of which are available upon request, are qualitatively similar to those reported in Tables 2.4 and 2.7.

tent with recent empirical depictions of trading at large banks, at least with respect to interbank deals.

The earliest studies of currency dealers, Lyons (1995) and Yao (1998a) found such an effect for interbank trades. Bjønnes and Rime's (2003) more recent study, however, finds this effect for direct interbank trades but not for brokered trades. The difference between the early and later studies seems likely to reflect a dramatic shift in interbank trading practice over the interval between studies. When Lyons' dealer was trading in 1992, interbank trading was mainly executed via direct interdealer communication and voice brokers. By the late 1990s interbank trading was dominated by electronic broker systems – primarily EBS and Reuters Dealing 2000-2 – that did not even exist in 1992. Since then, the fraction of interbank deals carried out through brokers has risen further.[22] Indeed, our dealer reports, consistent with other dealers at large banks, that the vast majority of his interbank trades are brokered. Since we cannot distinguish between direct and brokered trades, it is not surprising that we find no evidence of such an effect.

It is noteworthy that the coefficient on customer trade size is significant at the ten percent level. A significant effect would be consistent with the findings of other authors, including Bjønnes and Rime (2001a) and Yao (1998a) that trade size has a positive influence on spread for customer trades. Of course, a significant effect could reflect either prospective inventory costs or asymmetric information. We provide evidence later that there is a second-order positive relationship between trade size and spread for commercial customer trades, and that it likely reflects inventory considerations.

2.3.3 Influence of existing inventory

Our results indicate that existing inventory has no influence on the prices quoted to other dealers. The absence of any effect on prices to other dealers is consistent with results from other recent studies, such as Bjønnes and Rime (2003) and Yao (1998a).

By contrast, Lyons' (1995) provides clear evidence that his dealer engaged in price shading in 1992. However, Lyons dealer was a "jobber," an unusual type of dealer who deals exclusively with other dealers, at extremely high frequency. Yao (1998a) argues that his dealer's large customer business provided an information advantage, and that his dealer avoided price shading because it might signal his information to other dealers. The potential relevance of this motivation is underscored by Yao's complementary finding that the dealer clearly did shade prices to customers in response to inventory accumulation. Since customers are less likely to trade on information they glean from dealers, the costs of revealing information to them are relatively slight.

---

22   That is what Carpenter and Wang (2003) find in their study for the large interbank trades.

Bjønnes and Rime (2003) argue that the difference between their result and Lyons' may also reflect the shift towards brokered deals within interbank trading. These are both more convenient and more transparent than earlier methods of trading. Since dealers now have this attractive alternative approach to unloading unwanted inventory, they are no longer willing to give away information on their inventory position by shading quoted prices on incoming trades.

We find some evidence of modest price shading with respect to customers: quotes may be shaded one pip for every million dollars of inventory. However, the shading seems to go the "wrong" way: higher inventory leads to higher quoted prices. This contrasts with the findings of Yao (1998a) and Bjønnes and Rime (2001a), who find modest – or at least "correctly signed" – amounts of standard price shading for customer trades. Section 2.4 provides one possible explanation for this effect. We stress, however, that the apparent reverse price shading is slight.

2.3.4 Inventory management

This section documents that our dealer controls his inventory quite similarly to dealers at large banks. He keeps it close to zero, typically bringing it half-way back to zero within a quarter hour of an inventory shock, and primarily uses outgoing trades to manage the process. We undertake a simple autoregression of the dealer's inventory position:

$$I_t - I_{t-1} = \alpha + \beta I_{t-1} + \varepsilon_t. \tag{2}$$

If the dealer rigidly controls his inventory, true β is negative and close to unity in absolute value. If the dealer allows his inventory to change randomly, the true β is zero.

Our results, presented in Table 2.5 clearly show that the USD/EUR dealer at our small bank works consciously to keep inventories close to zero, though he does allow his inventory to vary somewhat. For the overall sample (all trades and all counterparties except preferred customers), β is negative and statistically significant at -0.17, implying a median inventory half-life of 17 minutes. This is quite close to the 18-minute median inventory half-life for the NOK dealer at the big bank studied in Bjønnes and Rime (2003), who did about 58 trades per day, similar to the 51 daily trades of our dealer. However, our dealer's median inventory half-life is far longer than the median half-lives of the three DEM/USD dealers at that bank, which varied from 0.7 to 3.7 minutes. These dealers, unsurprisingly, trade more frequently, averaging 85 to 200 trades per day.

Table 2.5 Mean reversion in dealer's EUR/USD inventory

Table shows results for the following inventory change regression:

$$I_t - I_{t-1} = \alpha + \beta I_{t-1} + \varepsilon_t,$$

where I_t represents the dealer's inventory level in millions of euros.

Sample:	β	Standard error	Implied mean half-lives (minutes)	Implied median half-lives (minutes)	Observations
All trades	***-0.17	0.006	58	17	3,534
All incoming trades	***-0.20	0.008	48	14	2,858
Incoming trades with:					
other banks	***-0.27	0.029	38	11	1,195
customers	***-0.33	0.020	31	9	1,663
commercial customers	***-0.35	0.044	30	9	1,492
financial customers	***-0.47	0.107	23	7	170

Since our dealer does not seem to shade quoted prices to adjust inventory, it is reasonable to suppose he uses the other dominant approach to inventory management: actively contacting other dealers through the interbank market (Bjønnes and Rime, 2003). To examine this possibility, we carry out a probit analysis of whether a given interbank trade is outgoing, in the spirit of Bjønnes and Rime (2003):

$$\text{Prob}(\text{Tr}_t = \text{OutIB}) = P[|I_t|, |I_t|^2, \text{Tr}_{t-1} = \text{InIB}|Q_{t-1}|, \text{Tr}_{t-1} = \text{FC}|Q_{t-1}|, \text{Tr}_{t-1} = \text{CC}|Q_{t-1}|, |Q_t|]$$

The absolute value of inventory at the beginning of each period, $|I_t|$, and its squared value should capture the possibility that a dealer will more quickly initiate an outgoing trade when he has more inventory risk. If dealers work more actively to eliminate large inventories than small ones, this variable will have a positive coefficient. If dealers automatically eliminate any inventory, this variable will have an insignificant coefficient.

The variables $\text{Tr}_{t-1} = \text{IB}|Q_{t-1}|$, $\text{Tr}_{t-1} = \text{FC}|Q_{t-1}|$, and $\text{Tr}_{t-1} = \text{CC}|Q_{t-1}|$ each refer to whether the previous trade was incoming, and distinguish among incoming trades from the three counterparty types, interbank, financial customer, and commercial customer, respectively, multiplied by the absolute value of that trade. The coefficients on these variables will be positive if outgoing trades are customarily used to eliminate unwanted inventory. We allow the coefficients to vary according to trade counterparty in case the relative information value of these customers' trades affects the perceived importance of eliminating inventory. For example, a sale initiated by another bank may indicate an imminent appreciation of the commodity currency, heightening the importance of eliminating the consequent short position immediately. A sale initiated by a commercial customer would have no implications for the likely direction of the exchange rate, and the dealer could therefore feel less pressure to eliminate the short position. The final right-hand-side variable, $|Q_t|$, captures the absolute value of the current trade.

The results indicate that the likelihood of an outgoing trade rises with the absolute amount of existing inventory (Table 2.6). This is consistent with the possibility that dealers are more strongly motivated to eliminate unwanted inventory by placing an outgoing order when the inventory begins to accumulate (see also Yao, 1998a). By contrast, Bjønnes and Rime (2003) find inventory size to be immaterial to the direction of trade for two of their four dealers. For the two remaining ones, dealers 3 and 4, the coefficient on inventory indicates that they, too, are more likely to submit limit orders when their inventory is high.

Our results also indicate that outgoing trades are more likely when the previous trade was an incoming interbank or financial customer trade. This may reflect the relatively weak informational situation of the small bank, which may be particularly anxious to eliminate inventory accumulated through trades with better informed counterparties. Finally, the positive coefficient on $|Q_t|$ indicates that the orders our dealer submits to the brokers tend to be larger than his average incoming trade. This suggests that the dealer sometimes collects inventory from small customer trades and then squares his position by submitting one relatively large outgoing order (see also Bjønnes and Rime, 2003).[23]

---

23 To make sure that our finding is not dominated by the extension of considering the counterparty of incoming trades, the regression of Bjønnes and Rime (2003) is reproduced exactly without changing our results, however (see Annex 2.5).

Table 2.6 Probit-regression of choice of incoming/outgoing trade

Probit regression of incoming/outgoing interbank trade decision. Incoming interbank trades are coded 0, while outgoing interbank trades are coded 1. I represents the level of inventory in millions of euros. $Tr_{t-1}=IB|Q_{t-1}|$ represents the absolute value of the previous trade if it was an interbank trade; $Tr_{t-1}=FC|Q_{t-1}|$ represents the absolute size of the previous trade if it was with a financial customer; $Tr_{t-1}=CC|Q_{t-1}|$ represents the absolute value of the previous trade if it was with a commercial customer; $|Q_t|$ represents the absolute size of the current deal. R^2 is McFadden's analog to ordinary R^2-measures. 3,534 observations.

$$\text{Prob}(Tr_t = \text{OutIB}) = P[|I_t|, |I_t|^2, Tr_{t-1}=IB|Q_{t-1}|, Tr_{t-1}=FC|Q_{t-1}|, Tr_{t-1}=CC|Q_{t-1}|, |Q_t|]$$

Variable	Coefficient	Std. errors	z-statistic
Constant	***-1.117	0.04	-28.25
Absolute inventory ($|I_t|$)	***0.032	0.01	3.21
Inventory squared ($|I_t|^2$)	***-0.001	0.00	-2.91
Absolute size of previous trade, if incoming interbank trade (EUR millions)	***0.088	0.02	3.62
Absolute size of previous trade, if financial customer trade (EUR millions)	*0.034	0.02	1.84
Absolute size of previous trade, if commercial customer trade (EUR millions)	-0.004	0.01	-0.35
Absolute size of the current deal $|Q_t|$ (EUR millions)	***0.032	0.01	4.14
McFadden's R^2			0.01

As a final test of whether the dealer prefers to adjust inventory through outgoing interbank trades, we examine the relationship between cumulative customer order flow and cumulative outgoing interbank flows. As shown in Figure 2.2, cumulative customer flows and outgoing interbank trades track each other quite closely. To substantiate this relationship statistically, we run a simple cointegrating regression:

$$\sum_{i=0}^{t} \text{Outgoing Interbank Trade}_i = \delta + \lambda\, \text{Trend} + \gamma \sum_{j=0}^{t} \text{Customer Trade}_j + \pi_t$$

The more the dealer uses outgoing interbank trades to unwind unwanted inventory position, the closer γ will be to unity. The results, shown below, support the importance of outgoing interbank trades as an instrument of inventory control (standard errors in parentheses):[24]

---

24 Standard Errors in parentheses.

$$\sum_{i=0}^{t} \text{Outgoing Interbank Trade}_i = 13.2 - 0.02\text{Trend} + 0.56 \sum_{j=0}^{t} + \pi_t$$
$$\phantom{\sum_{i=0}^{t}} \quad (0.41) \quad (0.00) \quad (0.01)$$

The adjusted R^2 for this regression is 0.90. The ADF test statistic for this regression is -3.97, and the Philips-Perron test statistic is -4.59; both are statistically significant at the 1 percent level.

Figure 2.2 Cumulative customer order flow and cumulative incoming and outgoing interbank order flow

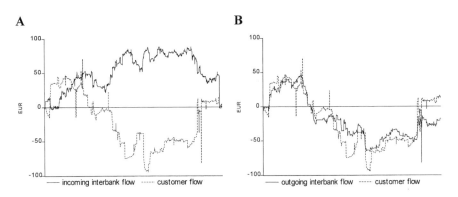

Plots show the evolution of cumulative customer order flow and cumulative incoming and outgoing interbank order flow, measured in EUR millions.

2.4 Spread variation across customers and trade size

So far our analysis shows that our small-bank dealer in USD/EUR behaves similarly to contemporaneous dealers at larger banks. To facilitate that comparison, however, we have not exploited of our ability to distinguish between financial and commercial customers. In this section we show that spreads differ strikingly across customer types and across trade sizes.

2.4.1 Financial and corporate customers

We next run the Lyons/Madhavan-Smidt model, incorporating the distinction between commercial and financial customers. The results indicate that banks distinguish sharply among customer types (Table 2.7).[25] The average half-spread on commercial customer trades is 10-pip, while the average half-spread on financial customer trades is only 2-pips. Indeed, the average half-spread on financial customer trades is only marginally significantly different from zero. Interestingly, average half-spreads on financial customer trades are not very different from those on interbank trades.

It is helpful to compare this pricing behavior with the behavior predicted by models of market-making under asymmetric information trading. In one set of models, dealers are assumed to take the amount of informed trading as exogenously determined (Copeland and Galai, 1983; Easley and O'Hara, 1987; Glosten and Milgrom, 1985). Since these are basically stock market models, the "information" involved is private information about the asset's fundamental value, and market makers always lose to informed traders. As in stock markets, market makers in these models cannot avoid informed traders, because they don't know their counterparties' identities. Thus, spreads would be widest for specific "informed" counterparties if their identities were revealed before trades occur.

By contrast, we show that currency dealers, who usually know the identity of their counterparties, provide the narrowest spreads for counterparties who are most likely to be informed. Market participants at large and small banks confirm this pattern of tiering across counterparties.[26] For example, Peter Nielsen, Global Head of Sales for the ROYAL BANK OF SCOTLAND Financial Markets, says:

"Large customers tend to get better prices than smaller customers as they generally have more banking relationships, thereby providing a greater facility for price discovery than smaller customers who may only have one banking counterparty. In addition, in general, larger transactions are quoted with tighter spreads than smaller transactions, although the large customers tend to receive best pricing for all business due to the buying power associated with their overall size and volume of business."

25 In order to identify an "unexpected component" of order flow Romeu (2003) suggests a modification which we have applied, too. It does bring about a correctly signed and statistically significant order flow term in some cases, indicating an asymmetric information effect, but not in all. Therefore, we do not follow up this approach here.

26 However, they indicate that the correct counterparty disaggregation is between small commercial customers, on the one hand, and financial customers and large multinational (commercial) corporations, on the other hand. Though we cannot distinguish between such commercial customers, our small bank is not likely to have done much business with large multinational corporations. Thus, the tiering by counterparty reported in Table 2.7 seems likely to capture the true tiering.

Table 2.7 Modified baseline model for different counterparty groups

The dependent variable of the below estimation equation is Δp_t, the change in price between two successive trades measured in pips. Q_t is order flow measured in EUR millions multiplied with a dummy variable for each counterparty group, i.e. other dealers, commercial or financial customers respectively. I_t is the dealer's inventory at time t multiplied with a dummy variable for each counterparty group. D_t is an indicator variable picking up the direction of the trade, positive for purchases (at the ask) and negative for sales (at the bid) again multiplied with a dummy variable for each counterparty group. Estimation uses GMM and Newey-West correction. Standard errors in the third column, and "***", "**" and "*" indicate significance at the 1%, 5% and 10%-level respectively.

$$\Delta p_t = \alpha + \beta_1 IBQ_t + \beta_2 FCQ_t + \beta_3 CCQ_t + IB(\gamma_1 I_t + \gamma_2 I_{t-1}) + FC(\gamma_3 I_t + \gamma_4 I_{t-1}) + CC(\gamma_5 I_t + \gamma_6 I_{t-1}) + \delta_1 IBD_t + \delta_2 IB(-1)D_{t-1} + \delta_3 FCD_t + \delta_4 FC(-1)D_{t-1} + \delta_5 CCD_t + \delta_6 CC(-1)D_{t-1} + \eta_t$$

Results for all incoming trades	Coefficient	Standard error
Constant	**-0.522	0.23
Order flow		
Interbank	-0.206	0.40
Financial customer	1.179	1.08
Commercial customer	0.679	0.44
Inventory		
Interbank trades	-0.270	0.35
Lagged	0.175	0.35
Financial customer trades	1.297	1.06
Lagged	-1.422	1.07
Commercial customer trades	**1.000	0.43
Lagged	**-1.079	0.43
Direction		
Interbank trades, current	***2.952	0.69
Lagged	***-1.517	0.48
Financial customer trades, current	***5.171	1.46
Lagged	*-2.114	1.17
Commercial customer trades, current	***11.906	0.52
Lagged	***-10.027	0.49
Adjusted R^2		0.23
Number of observations		2,859

There are at least three economic forces that could explain this counter-party-based tiering. First, it may partly reflect the relative elasticity of demand. Financial customer demand is likely to be more price elastic than commercial customer demand, since financial customers are better informed about the market. Financial customers often have access to the same quantity and quality of real-time trading information as the dealers themselves, and their deals are carried out by employees who specialize in trading. They incur these expenses because it is important to control their trading costs. By contrast, commercial customers (which are not multinationals) trade infrequently, do not incur the expense of real-time trading information systems and seldom employ foreign exchange specialists. They are less likely to know the opportunity cost of any given deal, and less likely to care if they do know it.

Second, counterparty-based tiering may be partly caused by efforts of banks to gain reputation from trading with "influential" big financial customers. The reputation bought here could be helpful in being accepted as a market maker in the interbank market and attracting business from commercial customers.

Third, counterparty-based tiering could also reflect asymmetric information. According to sources in the market, financial customer trades are generally considered far more "informative" than similarly-sized trades with commercial customers, and equally informative as trades with other dealers. Currency banks are known to value order flow for its information value. In essence, our bank may be effectively subsidizing the trades of counterparties in proportion to their information value. These subsidies would be intended to learn about the direction of financial customer flow and to encourage repeat business from the most informative counterparties.

A brief anecdote will underscore the seriousness with which banks pursue informative order flow. About a decade ago, a dispute arose between the salespeople and interbank traders at a significant foreign exchange dealing bank. The salespeople at this bank were spreading the quotes wider than the interbank traders thought proper. The salespeople's bonuses were based on the extent to which they "spread the quotes" wider than the quotes provided to them by the interbank dealers, so the salespeople were simply maximizing their own profits on a per-trade basis. The interbank traders, by contrast, wanted narrower spreads on certain types of deals, to encourage informative deal flow (they were explicit about the need to learn about the market from deal flow). The interbank traders won this dispute hands down: the bonus formulae were even revised to ensure that salespeople and interbank traders would be motivated by profits from the trading room as a whole. Spreads narrowed and currency trading volume picked up immediately.

2.4.2 Trade size

The market participants with whom we discussed this research highlighted an important non-linear relationship between trade size and spreads. For normal deals, meaning those below EUR 20 or 25 millions, larger trades usually receive better prices; above that cutoff the reverse is true. This pricing approach for normal deals essentially mimics the "volume discounts" of normal commerce. Since almost all the trades of our small bank fall under the 20-25 million cutoff, this input from dealers suggests that spreads at our bank should be wider for smaller deals.[27]

Dealers also indicated other dimensions of non-linearity in the pricing of normal-sized deals. For customer trades, banks typically distinguish three explicit but inexact size ranges. "Regular trades" vary from EUR 1 million to EUR 20-25 million. Any trade under that amount will be spread substantially wider, though the exact spread varies according to the bank's discretion. The smallest trades are priced according to a formula and typically carry an extremely wide spread: three percent is not considered an unreasonable.[28] For interbank trades the nonlinearity in pricing takes a different form. Since EBS trades must be EUR 1 million or larger, there may be a discontinuity in the price function at EUR 1 million.

With the benefit of these insights from the front lines, we modify the Lyons/Madhavan-Smidt model by allowing spreads to vary non-linearly by trade size. For financial and commercial customer trades we distinguish three size ranges: "large", meaning trades of EUR 1 million and above; "medium", meaning trades between EUR 0.5 million and EUR 1 million; "small", meaning trades smaller than EUR 0.5 million. For interbank trades we distinguish between trades above and below EUR 1 million. We do not distinguish "very large trades", meaning those above EUR 20 or 25 million, because our dataset includes so few.

The results (Table 2.8) confirm a strong negative relationship between baseline spreads and deal size. For interbank trades, the half-spread on large trades, 1.3 pips, is less than half the spread on small trades, 2.9 pips. For financial customers, half-spreads on large and medium-sized trades are not significantly different from zero, while the half-spread on the small trades is 5.5 pips.[29] The tiering is most pronounced for commercial customers, who pay an average half-spread of 2.9 pips on large trades, 8.4 pips on medium-sized trades, and 11.4 pips on small trades.

---

27 As noted earlier, the positive relationship between deal size and price above 25 million could reflect either "prospective inventory" concerns or asymmetric information. Market participants, when asked, favor the inventory explanation.

28 Years ago, the husband of one of the authors was assigned to write a computer program that would automatically price the smallest trades at a three percent spread.

29 This is consistent with a common complaint heard from dealers over the past decade or so, that good financial customers can trade almost for free.

Table 2.8 Extended baseline model with trades distinguished by size and counterparty group

The dependent variable is Δp_t, the change in price between two successive trades measured in pips. IBQ_t is order flow measured in EUR millions interacted with a dummy variable for interbank trades; FCQ is order flow interacted with a financial customer dummy, and CCQ is order flow interacted with a commercial customer dummy. I_t is the dealer's inventory at time t; we again interact this with dummy variables for each counterparty group; D_t is an indicator variable picking up the direction of the trade, positive for purchases (at the ask) and negative for sales (at the bid); this, too, is interacted with dummy variables for the three counterparty groups, and each of the three resulting interaction terms is then interacted with dummy variables for trade size; "SM" for small, "MED" for medium, and "LG" for large. Estimation uses GMM and Newey-West correction. Standard errors in the third column, and "***", "**" and "*" indicate significance at the 1%, 5% and 10%-level respectively.

$$\Delta p_t = \alpha + \beta_1 IBQ_t + \beta_2 FCQ_t + \beta_3 CCQ_t + IB(\gamma_1 I_t + \gamma_2 I_{t-1}) + FC(\gamma_3 I_t + \gamma_4 I_{t-1}) + CC(\gamma_5 I_t + \gamma_6 I_{t-1}) + \delta_1 IB_{LG} D_t$$
$$+ \delta_2 IB_{LG}(-1)D_{t-1} + \delta_3 IB_{SM+MED} D_t + \delta_4 IB_{SM+MED}(-1)D_{t-1} + \delta_5 FC_{LG} D_t + \delta_6 FC_{LG}(-1)D_{t-1} +$$
$$\delta_7 FC_{MED} D_t + \delta_8 FC_{MED}(-1)D_{t-1} + \delta_9 FC_{SM} D_t + \delta_{10} FC_{SM}(-1)D_{t-1} + \delta_{11} CC_{LG} D_t + \delta_{12} CC_{LG}(-1)D_{t-1} +$$
$$\delta_{13} CC_{MED} D_t + \delta_{14} CC_{MED}(-1)D_{t-1} + \delta_{15} CC_{SM} D_t + \delta_{16} CC_{SM}(-1)D_{t-1} + \eta_t$$

Results for all incoming trades	Coefficient	Standard error
Constant	-0.257	0.22
Order flow		
Interbank	-0.448	0.39
Financial customer	1.085	0.98
Commercial customer	**0.916	0.46
Inventory		
Interbank	-0.223	0.36
Lagged	0.163	0.36
Financial customer trades	0.996	0.96
Lagged	-1.135	0.96
Commercial customer trades	**0.993	0.41
Lagged	**-1.013	0.41
Direction		
Interbank trades, large	***3.869	0.74
Lagged	***-1.282	0.51
Interbank trades, small	1.429	1.22
Lagged	***-2.883	1.33
Financial customer trades, large	1.208	1.94
Lagged	0.509	1.81
Financial customer trades, medium	3.610	2.46
Lagged	-0.772	2.39
Financial customer trades, small	***9.247	2.49
Lagged	***-5.461	1.67
Commercial customer trades, large	***4.142	1.73
Lagged	***-2.947	1.27
Commercial customer trades, medium	***14.043	1.59
Lagged	***-8.410	1.64
Commercial customer trades, small	***12.811	0.57
Lagged	***-11.447	0.57
Adjusted R^2		0.24
Number of observations		2,859

41

We also find a strong positive *residual* relationship between deal size and spreads, but only for commercial customer trades. That is, we find that, conditional on the baseline spread for its size category, the specific spread charged on a given trade rises with trade size (Figure 2.3). As noted above, this positive residual relationship could be either an asymmetric information effect or a prospective inventory effect. Most of these trades are very small (see Table 2.3), so their information content is likely to be commensurately small. Consistent with this, commercial customer trades are not generally considered informative by market participants. In short, the conditional positive relationship between size and spread at our banks seems more likely to reflect inventory concerns than to reflect asymmetric information.

Once again, it is worth contrasting these results with those implied by models of non-strategic market making under asymmetric information. As noted by Easley and O'Hara (1987), market makers can reasonably assume that counterparties choosing to deal large amounts are more likely to be informed, so spreads should be wider for large trades. Sirri and Petersen (2003) show that spreads are indeed wider for larger trades in equity markets. Our result also appear quite different from Lyons' (1995) conclusion that spreads widen with deal size for his currency "jobber".

Figure 2.3   Estimated spreads for trades of different size and counterparties

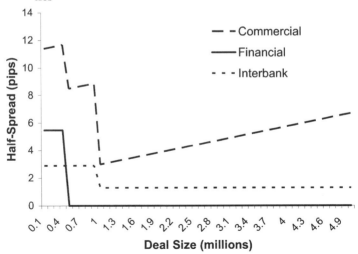

Plot shows estimated spreads for different counterparty groups according to trade sizes using the estimations in Table 2.8.

There are at least three reasons why banks may quote larger spreads on smaller currency trades. First, larger spreads ensure that small trades cover their fixed administrative costs of trading. As trades become smaller, these fixed costs represent a progressively larger proportion of the total deal size. Since currency market makers do not charge commissions, they recoup these costs by raising spreads. Second, small deals are relatively frequently placed by small commercial customers. These customers are generally less informed about current market prices than large customers, so their demand is presumably less price elastic. Third, there may be strategic reasons to narrow spreads on large deals. Large trades are usually placed by large customers, who are considered relatively "informed" by the dealers. With informed customers, there may be an incentive to encourage repeat business through price concessions.

2.4.3 Information in currency markets

What kind of information could dealers be trying to capture by subsidizing "informed" deal flow? Two alternatives roughly span the space: fundamental information, or information about transient aspects of trading.

Fundamental information

Abundant evidence indicates that order flow can affect financial prices. In stock markets, such evidence has been available at least since Shleifer (1986) noted that stock prices rise for firms added to the S&P 500 index (see also early Hasbrouck, 1991). Comparable evidence for currencies began to accumulate only around in the mid-1990s. Some studies analyzed as we do here the dealer's level of decision making, starting with Lyons (1995), others analyzed case study environments (Peiers, 1997; Ito, Lyons and Melvin, 1998; Rime 2000; Covrig and Melvin, 2002; Osler, 2003), news impact (Evans, 2002; Evans and Lyons, 2003); intervention impact (e.g. Dominguez, 2003; Payne and Vitale, 2003), or the use of flow analysis (Gehrig and Menkhoff, 2004). In particular, Lyons (2001a) and Fan and Lyons (2003) both find a strong positive correlation between exchange rates and cumulative financial order flow at a large bank (CITI-BANK), but no such relation with cumulative commercial customer order flow.

If informative order flow is subsidized at large banks then competition will force small banks to subsidize the same type of trades. It is not obvious, however, that the relatively limited order flow at a small bank would actually be informative. To examine the information value of our bank's order flow, we begin by plotting cumulative order flow against exchange rates for the three categories of incoming deals: interbank deals, financial customer deals, and commercial customer deals (Figure 2.4, A-C). In this exercise, we follow Lyons (2001a), Evans and Lyons (2002), Killeen, Lyons, and Moore (2001), and Fan and Lyons (2003). These figures suggest that there can be substantial information even in a small bank's order flow. Cumulative financial customer order flow tracks exchange rates quite clearly, and cumulative incoming interbank order flow tracks exchange rates even more closely.[30] Cumulative commercial customer order flow appears to have a negative relationship to exchange rates.

Figure 2.4   Price movements and cumulative order flows

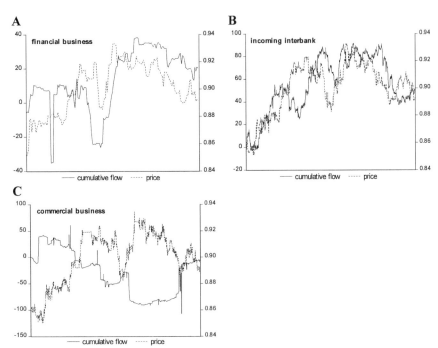

Plots show the evolution of price movements and cumulative order flows for different counterparties, i.e. commercial and financial customers, incoming interbank respectively, measured in EUR millions.

---

30   Given our finding presented in Section 2.3 that that cumulative commercial customer trades are strongly cointegrated with outgoing interbank trades, the negative relationship between exchange rates and cumulative commercial customer trade would seem to imply the negative relationship with cumulative outgoing interbank trades, and this is what we observe.

We formalize this analysis by estimating cointegrating relationships between exchange rates and our three categories of cumulative incoming order flow:

$$P_t = \omega + \phi trend + \sigma \sum_{j=0}^{t} CumulativeOrderFlow_j + noise_t$$

The results are consistent with our informal conclusions based on Figure 2.4: the USD/EUR exchange rate is strongly positively cointegrated with cumulative incoming interbank order flow: the cointegration coefficient, σ_{IB}, is quite significant at 0.503, and R_{IB}^2 is 0.47. The exchange rate is also moderately positively cointegrated with cumulative financial customer order flow: σ_{FC} is 0.434, with $R_{FC}^2 = 0.18$. Finally, the exchange rate is indeed negatively related to cumulative commercial customer order flow: σ_{CC} is -0.353, with $R_{CC}^2 = 0.57$. To investigate the possible role of deal size in communicating fundamental information, we focus on financial customer trades. We disaggregate these into small and "other" financial customer trades, since this seems to be where the line is drawn between negligible and substantial spreads (Table 2.8). Cointegration tests show that the link between cumulative financial customer order flow and exchange rate levels is significant for medium and larger trades ($\sigma_{MLFC} = 0.255$, $R_{MLFC}^2 = 0.20$) but insignificant for small trades. These results are consistent with the hypothesis that significantly-sized financial trades are quoted the tightest spreads in part because they have the highest fundamental-information value. Thus, it is plausible that large and medium-sized trades are subsidized the most in order to encourage future financial customer business. Commercial customer trades, which have essentially no information value, are quoted the widest spreads in part because they are "subsidized" the least.[31]

The literature provides evidence for at least two reasons the influence of order flow on financial prices could be permanent. First, order flow may reflect fundamental information about the asset's future value (Kyle, 1985; Glosten and Milgrom, 1985; Evans and Lyons, 2002; Payne, 2003). Second, an asset may face an underlying "downward-sloping demand" (Shleifer, 1986), due to risk aversion or differing information sets across investors. Though there is no reason to assume that only one of these would operate, our results seem to support the first connection over the second. In the presence of a downward sloping demand curve, commercial customer order flow would also be positively related to exchange rates.

---

31 One might argue that commercial order flow is truly informative, based on the strongly negative relationship between it and exchange rates. However, we interpret this relationship differently. Total deal flow in the market must sum to zero: the amount of sales must equal the amount of purchases. For some types of traders – like financial customers or banks as a group – to be influential, or to successfully anticipate the market, they must find counterparties who are not influential or who fail to anticipate the market. It appears that commercial customers fulfill this role.

These positive relationships between order flow and exchange rates fit the existing literature, but are nonetheless remarkable since they apply to a small dealer. Small dealers receive an order-of-magnitude less deal flow than large dealers. That a small dealer can recognize anything at all from incoming deals indicates that deal flow may be strongly correlated across locations and across bank types. Thus, information in the foreign exchange market may be widely and quickly disseminated.

Transient information

If a dealer were to gather fundamental information from observing customer trades, how would he use it? As described in Bjønnes and Rime (2001a), "If a dealer has good information from customer trades, it will be natural to utilize this information in his own position taking. After receiving a customer trade, the dealer may choose to place his own orders with other dealers, rather than to wait for others to contact him. This is important in foreign exchange markets, where the multiple dealership structure allows the dealers to trade actively in addition to functioning as market makers."

If the information is about fundamentals, then presumably the dealer will hold the position until the information is reflected in exchange rates. However, currency fundamentals tend to influence exchange rates extremely slowly. Empirical evidence shows that adjustment to fundamentals such as price levels takes many years (Rogoff, 1996). By contrast, currency dealers generally close out their positions before they go home for the day.

Indeed, it is not even clear whether there *could* be much truly "private information" about exchange rate fundamentals. The forces that drive currency markets are primarily macroeconomic in nature, and information about macroeconomic developments is largely public. Searching hard, one can identify two likely sources of "private" information held by currency market customers: specific FDI flows (What company is buying which other company? When?), and foreign exchange intervention. With respect to intervention, however, central banks typically guard their plans quite closely.[32] In stock markets, by contrast, individuals often learn specific information about corporations that may be relevant to their "true" values. Just visiting a company, or one of its competitors, can often be very enlightening. Informed trading is apparently of sufficient magnitude that the risk of such trading helps determine the cross-section of returns (Easley, Hvidkjaer and O'Hara, 2002).

We suggest that currency dealers may subsidize order flow from certain clients in order to learn information about transient aspects of trading. In particular, we note that currency order flow is correlated – there tend to be "runs" of

---

32 It is possible that certain market participants process the same public information with a better model, and arrive at more accurate predictions. However, accuracy in foreign exchange forecasting is never substantial.

buy orders and "runs" of sell orders (Goodhart, Ito and Payne, 1996). Banks clearly have an advantage if they know when a run is about to start or end. Since customers are one of the main sources of such runs, it could be strategically useful to encourage the business of those customers that are most likely to be involved.

There are at least three reasons why order flow could be correlated. Agents in currency markets have a general tendency to extrapolate trends (MacDonald, 2002), as a result of which a currency rise could produce a flurry of buy orders, and vice versa. Alternatively, the common use of technical analysis could create strongly correlated forecasts among certain groups of market participants at certain times. Chu and Osler (2004), for example, show that equity trading is extremely high when the market completes a "head-and-shoulders" chart pattern.

A third potential source of correlated order flow is particularly useful for illustrating the value of strategic dealing. It concerns dealers' standard approach to "working" extremely large deals (say, USD 100 million or more). In equity markets such deals are handled in a large, well-organized market for "block trades". In currency markets, the equivalent to this "upstairs market", an electronic system run by STATE STREET BANK called *Atriax*, is still in its infancy. Instead, a customer typically calls a bank and arranges to have the deal managed. Then the bank has all its dealers (regardless of their normal currency specialization) simultaneously get quotes from other dealers, and trade.[33] Other banks, ignorant of the true size of the deal, initially leave their quotes roughly consistent with previous market rates. However, once those other banks try to unload their new inventory, they discover that all the other banks are trying to do the same thing, and realize that prices must adjust.[34] The original dealing bank gets a good price for its customer, and the other dealing banks get hurt. Situations like this, which clearly produce correlated order flow, highlight the advantage of being the "informed" bank. A bank can presumably increase the likelihood of being the manager of large deals by generally providing excellent pricing to those customers most likely to do large deals. Banks also try to capture such business by entertaining such customers lavishly.

---

33 For the past two years or so, most interbank trades in major currencies are carried out through electronic brokers, so that calling other dealers directly now has strong signal value. As a result, the process for handling extremely large deals has changed, as well. Even though it works primarily through the brokers now, the basic strategy remains unchanged: get other market makers to quote and deal before information gets out about the true size of the overall trade.

34 Evans and Lyons (2003), who show that exchange rates respond to order flow, hypothesize that exchange rates respond to the fundamental information conveyed by order flow. Osler (2002) shows that exchange rates are affected by order flow even when it is not informative about market fundamentals. Lyons (2001a) provides further evidence consistent with the influence of non-informative order flow.

It is interesting to compare the incentives for strategic dealing in stock and currency markets. Why does strategic dealing lead to narrower spreads for informed trades in currency markets, but wider spreads for informed trades in stock markets? The reasons may stem from differences across markets in the benefits and costs of informed deal flow. The benefits from positioning based on order flow information may be larger in currency markets, since they are unregulated. Front running is (said to be) common practice in currency markets, but stock market dealers' are prohibited from engaging in the practice. In addition, specialists on the NYSE have no other dealers with whom they can trade, which makes it more difficult to manage the inventory risks associated with positions. Finally, the aggregate costs of dealing with informed traders may be larger in stock markets, where private information may be more prevalent, which would also discourage market makers in equity markets from subsidizing informed deal flow.

2.5 The asymmetric-information share of currency spreads

Though the costs of dealing with informed traders may be lower in currency markets than equity markets, those costs are not zero in either market. For example, currency dealers do need to worry that somebody else is managing the latest FDI transaction. This section provides evidence that the costs of dealing with "informed" counterparties do affect spreads in currency markets, even though they do not dominate them.

We implement one of the approaches to estimating spread components suggested in Huang and Stoll (1997). This model includes on the right-hand-side trades direction, D_t, the change in direction $D_t - D_{t-1}$, and existing inventory I_t:[35]

$$\Delta p_t = \frac{S}{2}(D_t - D_{t-1}) + \lambda \frac{S}{2} D_{t-1} - \delta \Delta I_t + e'_t \tag{3}$$

If existing inventories have no influence on spreads, then λ can be interpreted as the share of the asymmetric information component in total spreads.

We apply this model to our bank's trade data disaggregated according to counterparty and trade size (Table 2.9). Before we examine influence of asymmetric information on spreads, it is worth noting that our earlier findings receive strong confirmation: Average spreads are again smallest for interbank trades and highest for commercial customers. As before, we find clear evidence of tiering based on trade size, with smallest trades charged the widest spreads.[36] Finally, inventory concerns still seem to have little influence on spreads, though we still find the unexpected (negative) sign on inventories with respect to commercial customer trades.

---

35 The inventory component was actually introduced by Bjønnes and Rime (2003).
36 We have re-estimated the Huang-Stoll model of Table 2.9 in less disaggregated form, to correspond better with earlier literature; results fit nicely to earlier findings (Annex 2.6).

Table 2.9   Huang and Stoll (1997) indicator model with multiple trade sizes for counterparty groups

$$\Delta p_t = \frac{S}{2}(D_t - D_{t-1}) + \lambda \frac{S}{2} D_{t-1} - \delta \frac{S}{2} \Delta I_t + e_t'$$

The coefficients are estimated by GMM and Newey-West correction. Standard errors are reported in the third columns. Significance at the 1, 5 and 10 percent levels is indicated by ***, ** and *, respectively. The dependent variable Δp_t is the change in price between two incoming trades, measured in pips. ΔI_t is the change of inventory from t-1 to t. The adjusted R^2 stems from the same regression including a constant.

Dependent variable: Δp_{it}		
Variable	Coefficient	Std. error
Interbank half-spread (S/2), large trades	***3.934	0.75
Interbank half-spread (S/2), small trades	0.817	1.31
Financial customers half-spread (S/2), large trades	1.597	1.88
Financial customers half-spread (S/2), medium trades	**4.918	2.31
Financial customers half-spread (S/2), small trades	***9.304	2.44
Commercial customers half-spread (S/2), large trades	***4.478	1.65
Commercial customers half-spread (S/2), medium trades	***12.963	2.60
Commercial customers half-spread (S/2), small trades	***12.805	0.57
Interbank information (λ), large trades	***0.717	0.13
Interbank information (λ), small trades	-2.729	5.57
Financial customers information (λ), large trades	1.965	1.80
Financial customers information (λ), medium trades	*0.802	0.46
Financial customers information (λ), small trades	**0.391	0.19
Commercial customers information (λ), large trades	0.364	0.32
Commercial customers information (λ), medium trades	**0.348	0.15
Commercial customers information (λ), small trades	***0.101	0.02
Interbank inventory (δ), large trades	-0.077	0.06
Interbank inventory (δ), small trades	4.814	8.83
Financial customers inventory (δ), large trades	0.003	0.12
Financial customers inventory (δ), medium trades	-0.433	0.42
Financial customers inventory (δ), small trades	-0.046	0.20
Commercial customers inventory (δ), large trades	*-0.021	0.01
Commercial customers inventory (δ), medium trades	0.090	0.23
Commercial customers inventory (δ), small trades	*-0.072	0.04
Adjusted R^2	0.23	
Number of observations	2,859	

The news from these regressions concerns the share of the asymmetric information components of spreads. Though the results are not all conclusive, the coefficients generally indicate that, within size categories, the asymmetric information component is smaller for commercial customers than for financial customers. For example, the asymmetric information component is ten percent of the baseline spread on small commercial customer trades, but 39 percent of the baseline spread on small financial customer trades. Since commercial customer trades are generally considered less informative than financial customer trades, this result is consistent with the prediction that the asymmetric information component of spreads should be widest for trades with the most informed counterparties.

Similarly, the coefficients generally indicate that the share of the asymmetric information component rises with trade size, when we control for counterparty type. For example, point estimates of the asymmetric information component for small, medium, and large financial customer deals are 39 percent, 80 percent, and more than 1, respectively. The main ambiguity here concerns the asymmetric information component of spreads on the largest trades. While the coefficient values themselves are consistent with the pattern we present, they are measured very imprecisely, and are not statistically different from zero for either customer type.

In short, these results suggest that the costs of dealing with counterparties with private information do affect spreads in currency markets. The asymmetric information share of spreads is highest for counterparties that are most likely to be informed. However, the influence of these asymmetric information costs seems to be only secondary, overall, since the absolute size of spreads declines as counterparties become more informed.

2.6   Conclusions

This paper provides evidence that currency dealers strategically adjust spreads to maximize their deal flow from "informed" counterparties. Spreads are narrowest for relatively large deals with the most informed counterparties, specifically financial customers and other dealers. This outcome differs from the predictions of models of non-strategic dealing under asymmetric information (Copeland and Galai, 1983; Glosten and Milgrom, 1985; Easley and O'Hara, 1987). It is, however, consistent with the general notion of strategic dealing discussed in Gammill (1989) and Leach and Madhavan (1992).

We contrast currency markets with stock markets, where spreads seem to be widest for trades with the highest likelihood of representing informed counterparties. We suggest that the benefits of encouraging informed deal flow may be higher in currency markets, in part because they are unregulated. In addition, the costs of encouraging such deal flow may be smaller in currency markets, where truly private information is likely to be less prevalent. We also provide evidence, however, that the costs of asymmetric information are not zero, even in currency markets. Specifically, we show that the share of the asymmetric component of spreads tend to be larger for larger trades with more informed counterparties. That is, spreads for such deals are smaller, on average, but the share of the asymmetric component of such spreads is larger.

The underlying data comprise the complete USD/EUR trading record of a small German dealing bank over four months in 2001. These data have the advantage of distinguishing two types of customers, financial and commercial. Previous research on currency dealing has been unable to examine how this distinction affects spreads, for various reasons. To demonstrate that our results should apply to major foreign exchange markets overall, rather than just to our small bank, we show that the pricing and inventory management practices of our bank are congruent with such practices at large banks. The prevalence of the pricing practices we document is also attested to by players at major banks. This consistency of pricing across dealers makes economic sense, given the intensely competitive nature of currency markets.

Our analysis brings sharply into focus the need to understand the nature of information in currency markets. Dealers could be trying to maximize their inflow of either fundamental information or information concerning transient aspects of trading. We provide evidence that order flow may indeed provide fundamental information, but point out two reasons to question the relevance of such information for spreads. First, currency dealers' positions are usually closed out within a day. Second, there is probably far less "private fundamental information" in currency markets than in stock markets, since currency fundamentals are mostly macroeconomic aggregates and therefore publicly known.

We suggest that dealers may be concerned instead about transient information. Currency order flow is correlated – buys and sells come in runs. This pattern stems, at least in part, from the way dealers handle very-large trades, which exploits the fact that other dealers cannot know whether a given deal represents the beginning of a run. Thus, by subsidizing customers who tend to do large deals, the dealers may be maximizing their chances of managing the next very-large deal that comes along. The nature of "information" in currency markets is an important area for future research.

Annex 2.1   Lyons' baseline model for all incoming trades

The dependent variable of the below estimation equation is Δp_t, the change in price between two successive trades measured in pips. Q_t is order flow measured in EUR millions. I_t is the dealer's inventory at time t. D_t is an indicator variable picking up the direction of the trade, positive for purchases (at the ask) and negative for sales (at the bid). Standard errors are reported, and "***", "**" and "*" indicate significance at the 1%, 5% and 10%-level respectively.

$$\Delta p_t = \alpha + \beta Q_t + \gamma_1 I_t + \gamma_2 I_{t-1} + \delta_1 D_t + \delta_2 D_{t-1} + \eta_t$$

Variable	Interbank spot trades (GMM and Newey-West correction)	
	Coefficient	Standard Error
Constant	***-2.661	0.49
Order flow, Q_t	0.519	0.34
Inventory		
Current, I_t	-0.083	0.14
Lagged, I_{t-1}	0.045	0.13
Direction		
Current, D_t	***1.993	0.70
Lagged, D_{t-1}	***-1.829	0.49
Adjusted R^2		0.01
Number of observations		1,087

52

Annex 2.2 Modified baseline model for different counterparty groups – incoming spot trades only

The dependent variable of the below estimation equation is Δp_t, the change in price between two successive trades measured in pips. Q_t is order flow measured in EUR millions multiplied with a dummy variable for each counterparty group, i.e. other dealers, commercial or financial customers respectively. I_t is the dealer's inventory at time t multiplied with a dummy variable for each counterparty group. D_t is an indicator variable picking up the direction of the trade, positive for purchases (at the ask) and negative for sales (at the bid) again multiplied with a dummy variable for each counterparty group. Estimation uses GMM and Newey-West correction. Standard errors in the third column, and "***", "**" and "*" indicate significance at the 1%, 5% and 10%-level respectively.

$$\Delta p_t = \alpha + \beta_1 IBQ_t + \beta_2 FCQ_t + \beta_3 CCQ_t + IB(\gamma_1 I_t + \gamma_2 I_{t-1}) + FC(\gamma_3 I_t + \gamma_4 I_{t-1}) + CC(\gamma_5 I_t + \gamma_6 I_{t-1}) + \delta_1 IBD_t + \delta_2 IB(-1)D_{t-1} + \delta_3 FCD_t + \delta_4 FC(-1)D_{t-1} + \delta_5 CCD_t + \delta_6 CC(-1)D_{t-1} + \eta_t$$

Variable	Coefficient	Standard error
Constant	*-0.473	0.28
Interbank order flow	0.579	0.36
Financial customer order flow	-0.258	0.48
Commercial customer order flow	**-0.337	0.16
Inventory interbank trades	-0.199	0.15
Lagged	0.192	0.16
Inventory financial customer trades	-0.267	0.45
Lagged	0.284	0.48
Inventory commercial customer trades	-0.056	0.10
Lagged	-0.017	0.09
Interbank direction	0.775	0.72
Interbank direction, lagged	**-1.225	0.53
Financial customer direction	***5.865	2.23
Financial customer direction, lagged	***-4.261	1.35
Commercial customer direction	***11.746	0.56
Commercial customer direction, lagged	***-9.555	0.51
Adjusted R^2	0.23	
Number of observations	2,219	

Annex 2.3 Modified baseline model for different counterparty groups – for subperiods (months)

The dependent variable of the below estimation equation is Δp_t, the change in price between two successive trades measured in pips. Q_t is order flow measured in EUR millions multiplied with a dummy variable for each counterparty group, i.e. other dealers, commercial or financial customers respectively. I_t is the dealer's inventory at time t multiplied with a dummy variable for each counterparty group. D_t is an indicator variable picking up the direction of the trade, positive for purchases (at the ask) and negative for sales (at the bid) again multiplied with a dummy variable for each counterparty group. Estimation uses GMM and Newey-West correction. Standard errors in the third column, and "***", "**" and "*" indicate significance at the 1%, 5% and 10%-level respectively.

$$\Delta p_t = \alpha + \beta_1 IBQ_t + \beta_2 FCQ_t + \beta_3 CCQ_t + IB(\gamma_1 I_t + \gamma_2 I_{t-1}) + FC(\gamma_3 I_t + \gamma_4 I_{t-1}) + CC(\gamma_5 I_t + \gamma_6 I_{t-1}) + \delta_1 IBD_t + \delta_2 IB(-1)D_{t-1} + \delta_3 FCD_t + \delta_4 FC(-1)D_{t-1} + \delta_5 CCD_t + \delta_6 CC(-1)D_{t-1} + \eta_t$$

Variable	Coefficient	Std. error	Coefficient	Std. error	Coefficient	Std. error	Coefficient	Std. error
Constant	***-1.52	0.58	-0.42	0.37	0.26	0.51	-0.40	0.48
Interbank order flow	**1.51	0.62	*-1.51	0.84	0.49	0.92	**2.26	0.96
Financial customer order flow	0.94	1.56	-0.01	0.56	-1.63	1.82	***-9.02	2.57
Commercial customer order flow	**2.12	0.88	-0.19	0.69	-1.29	0.99	0.41	0.75
Inventory interbank trades	0.60	0.62	*-1.27	0.77	-0.04	0.41	0.13	0.68
lagged	-0.83	0.59	1.21	0.78	0.08	0.40	-0.17	0.64
Inventory financial customer trades	1.00	1.49	0.05	0.55	-1.34	1.35	***-4.75	1.73
lagged	-0.24	1.45	-0.27	0.58	1.28	1.42	***7.43	2.44
Inventory commercial customer trades	***3.19	0.93	0.24	0.67	-0.02	0.91	0.58	0.74
lagged	***-3.23	0.95	-0.28	0.69	0.08	0.91	-0.69	0.75
Interbank direction	-0.84	1.28	***4.71	1.14	**3.68	1.58	*-2.93	1.50
Interbank direction, lagged	-1.75	1.13	-1.35	0.88	***-2.59	0.97	-0.82	0.88
Financial customer direction	*7.67	4.07	**4.91	2.40	4.46	3.69	***15.31	3.59
Financial customer direction, lagged	***-8.68	3.32	3.48	2.82	-0.46	1.69	***-8.30	2.14
Commercial customer direction	***14.28	1.28	***10.14	0.90	***13.05	1.18	***12.00	0.91
Commercial customer direction, lagged	***-11.09	0.96	***-9.065	0.79	***-11.08	1.36	***-10.68	0.87
Adjusted R^2		0.30		0.18		0.17		0.23
Month		Jul 01		Aug 01		Sep 01		Oct 01 – Nov 01
Number of observations		459		911		715		774

Annex 2.4 Modified baseline model for different counterparty groups – for trades within an inter-transaction time of 15 minutes

The dependent variable of the below estimation equation is Δp_t, the change in price between two successive trades measured in pips. Q_t is order flow measured in EUR millions multiplied with a dummy variable for each counterparty group, i.e. other dealers, commercial or financial customers respectively. I_t is the dealer's inventory at time t multiplied with a dummy variable for each counterparty group. D_t is an indicator variable picking up the direction of the trade, positive for purchases (at the ask) and negative for sales (at the bid) again multiplied with a dummy variable for each counterparty group. Estimation uses GMM and Newey-West correction. Standard errors in the third column, and "***", "**" and "*" indicate significance at the 1%, 5% and 10%-level respectively.

$$\Delta p_t = \alpha + \beta_1 IBQ_t + \beta_2 FCQ_t + \beta_3 CCQ_t + IB(\gamma_1 I_t + \gamma_2 I_{t-1}) + FC(\gamma_3 I_t + \gamma_4 I_{t-1}) + CC(\gamma_5 I_t + \gamma_6 I_{t-1}) + \delta_1 IBD_t + \delta_2 IB(-1)D_{t-1} + \delta_3 FCD_t + \delta_4 FC(-1)D_{t-1} + \delta_5 CCD_t + \delta_6 CC(-1)D_{t-1} + \eta_t$$

Variable	Coefficient	Standard error
Constant	**-0.473	0.21
Interbank order flow	**0.810	0.32
Financial customer order flow	0.291	0.86
Commercial customer order flow	0.517	0.40
Inventory interbank trades	***0.495	0.18
Lagged	***-0.596	0.17
Inventory financial customer trades	0.369	0.85
Lagged	-0.441	0.85
Inventory commercial customer trades	**0.792	0.37
Lagged	**-0.890	0.37
Interbank direction	***2.814	0.66
Interbank direction, lagged	***-2.013	0.45
Financial customer direction	***5.384	1.33
Financial customer direction, lagged	**-2.370	1.05
Commercial customer direction	***11.231	0.55
Commercial customer direction, lagged	***-10.083	0.56
Adjusted R^2	0.31	
Number of observations	1,938	

Annex 2.5   Probit-regression of choice of incoming/outgoing trade

Probit regression of incoming/outgoing interbank trade decision. Incoming interbank trades are coded 0, while outgoing interbank trades are coded 1. R^2 is McFadden's analog to ordinary R^2-measures. 3,534 observations.

$$\text{Prob}(Tr_t = \text{OutgoingIB}) = P[\text{Abs}(I_t), (I_t)^2, |Q_t|]$$

Variable	Coefficient	Std. Errors	z-Statistic
Constant	***-1.080	0.04	-28.49
Absolute inventory ($|I_t|$)	***0.034	0.01	3.47
Inventory squared ($|I_t|^2$)	***-0.001	0.00	-3.05
Absolute value of order flow $|Q_t|$	***0.033	0.01	4.32
McFadden's R^2			0.01

Annex 2.6 Results for the Huang and Stoll (1997) indicator model. Regressions of Δp_t between all incoming trades. Components of the spread in Panel A

$$\Delta p_t = \frac{S}{2}(D_t - D_{t-1}) + (\lambda + \delta)\frac{S}{2}D_{t-1} + e_t$$

Components of the spread in Panel B

$$\Delta p_t = \frac{S}{2}(D_t - D_{t-1}) + \lambda\frac{S}{2}D_{t-1} - \delta\frac{S}{2}\Delta I_t + e_t'$$

The coefficients are estimated by GMM and Newey-West correction. Standard errors are reported in the third columns. ***, ** and * indicate significance at the 1, 5 and 10 percent levels, respectively. The dependent variable Δp_t is the change in price between two incoming trades. ΔI_t is the change of inventory from t-1 to t. The adjusted R^2 stems from the same regression including a constant.

A   Results for HS baseline model, adverse selection and inventory costs not separated.

Variable	Coefficient	Standard error	Bjønnes and Rime (2003), dealer 2-3	Lyons (1995)
Half-Spread (S/2)	***6.609	0.35	***1.58	***1.74
Info. and inv. $(\lambda+\delta)$	***0.213	0.04	***0.78	***0.49
Adjusted R^2		0.13	0.09	0.18
Number of observations		2,859	914	838

B   Results for HS model, adverse selection and inventory costs separated.

Variable	Coefficient	Standard error	Bjønnes and Rime (2003), dealer 2	Lyons (1995)
Half-Spread (S/2)	***7.002	0.37	***1.46	***1.43
Information (λ)	***0.244	0.04	***0.72	***0.43
Inventory (δ)	***-0.049	0.01	0.00	***0.21
Adjusted R^2		0.13	0.03	0.20
Number of observations		2,859	430	838

3   Profit Sources in FX Trading*

3.1   Introduction

Microstructure research in foreign exchange markets is presently seen by many as an important avenue due to the "failure of the macro approach" (Flood and Taylor, 1996, Lyons, 2001a). Our deeper understanding of processes in foreign exchange is hampered, however, by limited data availability. In particular, profitability is a key source of information to understand the business but useful profit figures are extremely rare. We contribute to the literature by analyzing a new data set which brings about three novel features: first, it is possible to apply an event study approach when examining profitability of speculative FX position taking. Second, the data allow the distinction between different customer groups in FX markets. Third, the sample period of four months is long enough to identify systematic sources of profitability. As a result, we cannot find speculation contributing to the bank's trading profits. Also, interbank dealing does not generate any profits for our bank, so customer business is the only profit source. Among customer groups, larger commercial customers are most profitable in absolute terms as well as per trade.

The issue of trading profitability may be interesting by itself, but it is also a core element of Friedman's (1953) proposition that profitable speculation would be stabilizing. So, do banks' FX profits stem from heavy speculation which is at the same time profitable and stabilizing? Available studies do not really support this view: Fieleke (1981) cannot find that monthly foreign currency positions taken by US banks and non-banks would become profitable due to favorable exchange rate changes. The analysis of extended and weekly data for big players leads to the same results (Wei and Kim, 1997). Finally, available evidence from Lyons (1998) and Yao (1998b) on tick-by-tick trading data of two large banks identifies position taking as a minor source of profits. This latter evidence is quite limited, however, as it is based on one week of trading and five weeks respectively, a disadvantage in identifying a volatile phenomenon (Lyons, 1998). Further shortcomings are rooted in identifying volumes and prices of speculative trades. So at this stage of knowledge, there is still an obvious need for better data and more reliable approaches.

Moreover, where do profits come from, if not mainly from speculation? There are two further sources, one is the intermediating function in the interbank market and the other is customer business (Braas and Bralver, 1990, Yao, 1998b). Lyons' dealer (1998) trades in the interbank market only, so his profits

---

*   I would like to thank my co-author Lukas Menkhoff (University of Hannover, Germany). We are deeply indebted to the bankers who provided the data and discussed findings with us.

are mainly generated by earning minimal spreads from a very short-term jobbing approach. Yao's dealer (1998b) by contrast is also active in customer business and earns money from spreads given to commercial and financial customers. Both banks are very large, however, their trading volume being many times higher than at our comparatively small bank. Can the smaller bank also make money from these sources? According to a qualitative study by Braas and Bralver (1990) on profit sources in trading rooms, smaller banks are expected to make profits in customer business only, in particular with smaller customers (p.89).

These studies basically provide the state of knowledge which is expanded by the new data which allow for the application of more reliable approaches. We find that the small bank earns considerable revenues and – going beyond earlier calculations by distinguishing both – also makes profits. Moreover, we introduce new ways to identify revenues from speculative FX trading: the application of an event study method shows that speculative positions are tentatively built up after some momentum in exchange rates but fail to become profitable over the following 30 minutes. The spread analysis of interbank and customer business reveals that there is no room left for revenues from speculation. Also, the suggestion that exchange rate volatility would foster speculative profits cannot be confirmed by our case. Finally, when putting suggested determinants of profitability in a multivariate approach, it is just customer business that emerges as a significant profit source. So, the finding in the literature that speculation may contribute to FX trading profits (Lyons, 1998; Yao, 1998b) is not confirmed by our examination of a longer sample.

When analyzing customer business in more detail it is found that commercial customers are more profitable in absolute as well as in relative terms than financial customers. The opposite poles in this respect are the large trade with both groups: the spread with large financial customers is about zero, so no profits are made in this business despite large volumes. By contrast, about 72% of total profit is generated by large commercial customers. Although spreads are small with this group – in the order of about 3 basis points – the high volume in combination with negligible administrative costs leads to the high profitability found.

The paper proceeds as follows. Section 3.2 introduces into the data used. Then, Section 3.3 presents overall revenues and profits of the dealer's FX trading. Section 3.4 focuses on identifying possible revenues from speculation, whereas Section 3.5 analyzes profits disaggregated according to several sources. Section 3.6 concludes.

3.2   Data

The data set employed in this study consists of the complete USD/EUR trading record of a bank in Germany. The record covers 87 trading days, beginning on Wednesday, the 11th of July 2001, and ending on Friday, the 9th of November 2001. Compared with the other microstructure data sets mentioned (Lyons, 1998; Yao, 1998b), this is the longest observation period to date. Due to the size of the bank as a marginal market-making participant with a limited customer base, the transaction frequency is comparatively low. The bank realizes about 41 USD/EUR trades per day, including all kinds of transactions, whereas the big market makers covered earlier perform several times as many transactions per day. These kinds of calculations are performed for the bank and not for a single dealer. However, due to the comparatively small size of our institution, there is only one dealer responsible for the bank's USD/EUR inventory position and trading policy – although he may be supported by other dealers when required – so that there is no de facto difference to earlier studies covering dealers.

In order to obtain a broad data set, we include outright-forward trades in an adjusted manner, i.e. by correcting for the forward points. In our opinion, these trades should not be disregarded, as we especially focus on customer trading, and outright-forward trades account for a large portion of customer business. Moreover, outright-forward trades influence the inventory position in our bank, as this trading is also conducted by, and accounted for, the same dealer as the spot trading.

The data set consists of all trades, including indirect trades executed by voice-brokers or electronic brokerage systems such as EBS, direct trades completed by telephone or electronically, internal trades and customer trades. For trade size of one million EUR or more in the interbank market, the bank almost solely uses the electronic brokerage system EBS, because communication and transactions require less time than in any other interdealer trading channel. Moreover, spreads are very advantageous – around one or two pips only. All trades are entered manually into the "deals blotter" by the back-office without differentiating between the several trading channels of each transaction. Bid-offer quotes at the time of each transaction are not recorded, either, but we can easily identify bid-offer prices afterwards by means of the trade-initiating party. For each trade, the following information is obtained from the hardcopy record: (1) the type of each trade; (2) the date and time of the trade; (3) the counterparty; (4) the quantity traded; (5) the transaction price; (6) the forward points if applicable; (7) the initiator of the trade.

Identifying the initiator of each trade allows for distinguishing between incoming (passive) and outgoing (active) trades. Similar to the finding by Yao (1998b, Table 3b), approximately 53% of all trades are signed as incoming or passive.

Table 3.1 presents some statistics about the trades with different counterparties. The structure of the interdealer trades is very similar to the ones observed by Bjønnes and Rime (2003, Table 2). Of more interest may be the customer trades. The share of customer trading volume, amounting to nearly 37% (21% spot trades only), is striking. Moreover, our data set allows us to distinguish between two different groups of customers according to the bank's classification: financial business and commercial business. Whereas commercial customers mostly trade small positions in foreign exchange, financial customers transact larger amounts. The latter, however, trade less often with our bank than commercial customers.

Table 3.1   Types of trades

The table shows the EUR/USD trading activity of a small bank in Germany over the 87 trading days between July 11th, 2001, and November 9th, 2001. Preferred commercial customer trades are excluded.

| | All trades | All trades | | All customer trades | |
		Interbank	Cus-tomer	Financial business	Commercial business
Number of trades	3,539	1,876	1,663	171	1,492
(per cent)	100	53	47	10	90
Value of trades (millions)	4,122	2,536	1,586	405	1,181
(per cent)	100	62	38	(26)	(74)
Mean size (millions)	1.20	1.42	0.95	2.37	0.79
Median size (millions)	0.58	1.00	0.10	0.76	0.08

Finally, some cases are deleted from the final data set due to extreme price changes of more than 100 basis points or tiny volumes of less than 1,000 USD, as both characteristics may blur the relationships of interest. The final data set is thus composed of all incoming and outgoing spot and out-right-forward trades of the interdealer, the financial and the commercial customer business.

3.3   Overall revenue and profit

Due to the complete trading record being available, there is the chance to infer total revenues. The only assumption that has to be made – according to Lyons (1995) – is to set the open position at the start and the end of the day to zero. In fact, there are small open positions at the end of the day and it is unclear whether they are kept (partially) until next day or closed during the night. Nevertheless, these open positions are about 1 mill. EUR at the median and thus smaller than the median during the day which is about 3 mill. EUR. So, with the final open position artificially closed every day without profit or loss, the overall revenue during the 87-days period sums up to 966 thd. EUR.

This "hard" fact can be set in relation to the conceptually similar studies of Lyons (1998) and Yao (1998b). Table 3.2 gives comparative information on these studies. Our dealer works for a small FX trading bank where trading volume per day is 50 mill. EUR per day and thus a fraction of Lyons' 1,400 and Yao's 1,500 mill. USD per day. This corresponds with trades per day which is 41 for the small dealer, and 344 or 181 respectively for the big ones. Despite this underprivileged position, revenue figures of the small dealer are closer to the large competitors: revenue per day is 11 thd. EUR and, thus, only about 11% of Lyons' dealer, but 66% of Yao's dealer. When revenue per volume is considered, the gross "margin" of 2.23 basis points, i.e. in hundreds of per cent, is markedly higher than the 0.73 and 0.11 basis points for the large dealers. This higher margin is enough to compensate for the smaller trade size as revenue per trade is 268 EUR and thus about the same as 295 USD for Lyons' dealer and even ahead of the 94 USD for Yao's dealer.

Table 3.2   Revenue data of three banks

	This paper		Lyons (1998)	Yao (1998b)
	in EUR	in USD	in USD	in USD
Revenue (thousands)	966	867	508	424
Days considered	87	87	5	25
Revenue per day (thousands)	11.1	10.0	101.6	17.0
Trading volume (millions)	4,335	3,699	6,969	38,217
Trading volume per day (millions)	50	43	1,394	1,529
Revenue per volume (basis points)	2.23	2.34	0.73	0.11
Number of trades	3,609	3,609	1,720	4,518
Number of trades per day	41	41	344	181
Revenue per trade	268	240	295	94
Revenue per day (thousands)				
Minimum	-18	-17	40	-140
Maximum	70	63	200	150

It is well-known from the two earlier studies that trading revenues vary enormously from day to day and that they can be even negatively. Yao's dealer for example made losses on eight of the 25 trading days covered in the study (Yao, 1998b, Table 5). It is thus no surprise that the small dealer is also confronted by quite different daily successes. Figure 3.1 plots daily revenues with daily trading volume. One can directly see that there are many days with losses (20 out of 87). Moreover, revenue is generally positively related with volume, although not in a very strict way.

Figure 3.1 Daily trading volume and daily revenues

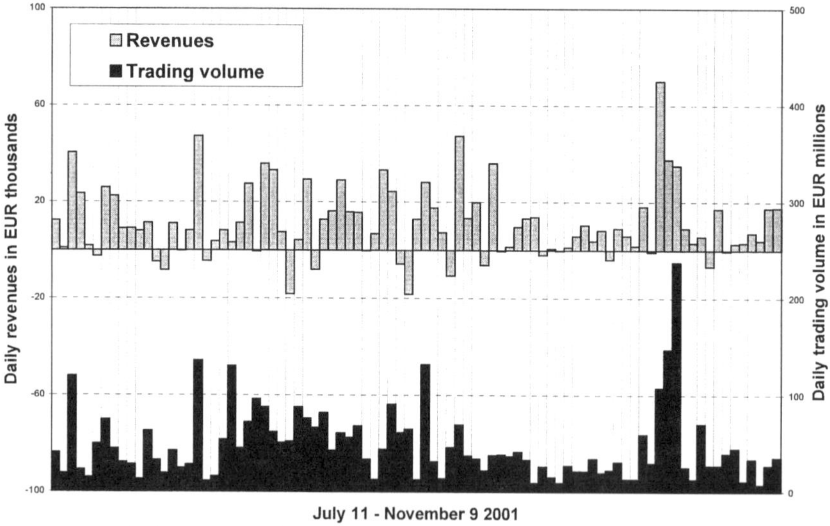

July 11 - November 9 2001

Figure shows daily overall trading revenues measured in EUR thousands and daily trading volume measured in EUR millions for all trades, i.e. interbank, financial and commercial customer trades, over the whole sample period (07/11/01 – 11/09/01).

In a last step, it seems worthwhile to calculate not just revenues but also profits. This requires at a minimum some information about administrative costs. Interviews in several trading rooms have shown that FX trading costs are preferably calculated as costs per trade, largely independent of the trade's size. The costs per trade mentioned by market participants are definitely influenced by several bank-specific factors but to operate with a concrete figure, the most often-mentioned figure for full costs is 100 EUR per trade. Again, it is not fully revealed which costs are covered by this figure, whether equity capital costs and risk costs are considered, to which extent overhead costs are included etc. However, the figure appears to be useful and it shows that FX trading at our bank does not only generate revenues but also profits: revenues per trade are 268 EUR on average compared to costs of 100 EUR which yields a profit of 606 thd. EUR for the four-month period. The cost per trade also indicates that the five weeks trading of Yao's dealer were most probably at the borderline of profitability.

So, revenues and even profits are earned on most days of our dealer's FX trading. This raises the question whether speculative position-taking of traders contributes to this result.

3.4 Revenues from the trader's speculation

3.4.1 Approaches identifying revenues from speculation

The question whether banks really earn money from their speculative FX trading has been examined by three approaches in the literature: first, position taking is analyzed, in particular position taking is related with later price changes. Second, due to difficulties in identifying speculative trades, speculative revenues have been regarded as the residual beyond revenues from customer and interbank trades. Third, it has been suggested that speculation will be more profitable in a volatile environment. We will follow these three approaches in Sections 4.2 to 4.4 by analyzing our new data set. What are plausible ex ante-explanations on speculative profits that can be drawn from empirical exchange rate studies?

The overwhelming finding of the literature is that there is no economic model to explain exchange rate movements at shorter-term horizons (Frankel and Rose, 1995; Kilian and Taylor, 2003). So, one would not really expect to see profits from position taking at monthly or weekly horizons. Fieleke (1981) uses the foreign currency positions of US firms that have to be reported to the US authorities on a monthly basis. The main analysis compares these open positions with later exchange rate changes and does not find a systematic relationship. The later work of Wei and Kim (1997) re-lies on an extended data base which also includes open positions resulting from currency business and which is available on a weekly basis. This data comprises 36 large players only, effectively the leading trading banks. So, if there is respective private information in the foreign exchange market, it might be revealed by analyzing the open positions of these large players over horizons between one day and 12 weeks. However, the result is quite similar to Fieleke (1981), despite more comprehensive, shorter-term data on the best informed market participants.

Empirical exchange rate research has found, however, two other starting-points for possibly profitable exchange rate speculation, i.e. the very long and the very short end of the market. At the long end, exchange rates show some tendency towards behaving in accordance with the purchasing power parity (Rogoff, 1996; Taylor, 2003). The necessary horizon of years is too long for most FX professionals but may explain why central banks tend to make money from interventions (Sweeney, 1997).

At the very short end, order flow has been revealed as a measure which transports private information (Ito, Lyons and Melvin, 1998; Covrig and Melvin, 2003; Osler, 2003; and Payne, 2003). Cumulated order flow is moreover related to exchange rate changes (e.g. Evans and Lyons, 2002; Fan and Lyons, 2003). So, if a bank had private information about future order flow, it could profit from this knowledge (see Braas and Bralver, 1990). In line with this insight into order flow it has been established that banks mostly speculate intra-day but square their positions at the end of the day. It is thus a necessary consequence to analyze high-frequency data if one would like to learn about possible profits from banks' speculation.

The first study analyzing such intra-day transaction data is Lyons (1998). He has the trading record data of a very large dealer over one week, generating total revenues of 508 thd. USD. To estimate the speculative profit, Lyons proposes two approaches. First, the total bid-ask spread in incoming orders is decomposed, ac-cording to the dealer's opinion, into two thirds for laying off the inventory shock and one third remaining revenue from interbank trading (there is no customer trading). This procedure leads to the necessarily imprecise result that intermediation explains more than 90% of total revenue. Thus speculation – as the residual – explains less than 10%. The second procedure is quite different: here, an instrument is suggested to define that part of inventory that is of speculative nature. This instrument is non-dealt quotes, which contain useful information about past price changes and help the dealer to determine his speculative demand. These non-dealt quotes can explain about one quarter of the dealer's position, i.e. the speculative part according to this argument. In the next step, Granger causality tests are performed in order to see whether speculative position forecasts price changes (Lyons, 1998, p.111). Finally, the value of the speculative position over time is measured. Neither step can identify profitable speculation: speculative positions neither Granger cause price changes nor is there an indication that speculative positions become more valuable over time, rather the opposite. This identification of speculative position holding may be imprecise, however, as other available information, such as further quotes in the market, volumes, conversations or transactions from voice brokers (that can be known), are not considered.

Another critique of Yao (1998b) brought forward against this approach is that the decomposition of inventory does not identify the quantity of speculative trading. He thus suggests another measure to identify speculation, i.e. trades that are initiated by the dealer and lead to an increase in inventory, so-called accumulating trades. This definition encompasses 4.2% of total trading volume of his bank (Yao, 1998b, p.24). Speculative profits are, however, calculated as a residual, having first measured revenue from customer trading and interbank or brokered business and subtracting these other revenue sources from actual total revenues. In essence, speculative revenue makes up for 28.5% of total revenue for this bank. However, this approach requires the precise identification of trades which close open positions from customer business in order to get spread information. This exact identification is impossible in a strict sense as inventory does not react fully and immediately. So there is room for interpretation about the "true" customer spreads and thus, finally, about the residual of speculative profits.

In summary, even high-frequency data are confronted with the identification problem that inventories at the same time reflect intermediation of interbank or customer orders as well as speculative position taking. It is thus most important to identify speculative trades without interference, for example by accumulating trades that increase inventory (Yao, 1998b). Then the profitability of speculative positions should be studied at short-term horizons. It remains to be seen whether this, as well as other approaches, confirms the finding of Lyons (1998) and Yao (1998b), that speculation contributes a share of between 0 and 30% to overall revenues.

3.4.2 Revenues from accumulating inventory?

The basic idea in identifying revenues from speculative trading has been to connect position-taking with later price changes. As discussed above, a conservative but reliable way is to take accumulating (outgoing) interbank trades. Its disadvantage is the narrow focus, but one can argue that if the dealer has forecasting ability and if he increases his open positions, then these trades should yield revenues over time. This leaves the possibility open that one is missing other sources of speculation.

We have thus conducted an event study in the sense that whenever the dealer at our bank accumulates inventory via an interbank trade, i.e. at time t=0, price changes before and after this decision are analyzed. In accordance with Yao (1998b) the data are cleaned for cases where the bank obviously increases inventory to serve a later customer order. Regarding the time horizon, one has to consider the short-term orientation of FX dealers. Half-lives of open positions are in the range of minutes only, in the case of our dealer it is about 15 minutes (see Mende and Menkhoff, 2003a). We decide to take twice the half-life, i.e. a time horizon of 30 minutes before and after engagement into a speculative trade.

In order to analyze price changes before and after the accumulating trades the prices available from our main data base are not sufficiently frequent and not easy to compare due to the different counterparties. Thus minute-by-minute quoted midpoint data have been taken, which serve as a reasonably close approximation of the alter-natives for our bank. We match both data bases by adjusting the accumulating trade to the market quotes: the matching mostly fits by the minute stamped but sometimes there seems to be an obvious late time-stamp due to some delay in the back office (see Section 3.2). In these latter cases the time is corrected by one or two minutes to better match market prices. Finally, exchange rate returns based on the midpoint quotes are calculated in a time window of 30 minutes before and after t=0.

Figure 3.2 presents results, differentiated for four origins of accumulating inventory, A to D: A shows returns for purchases conducted by outgoing trades only, B shows it for sells. C and D present returns when purchases and sells were conducted by incoming trades. The latter had not been considered by Yao (1998b) as incoming trades are initiated by the counterparty in the setting of direct trades. Our bank, however, relies for larger interbank trades almost exclusively on the electronic brokerage system, so that placing of a limit order can be seen as willingness to accept open positions at attractive prices. Whatever approach is taken, the result is always the same: there is no indication that this dealer would be able to accumulate inventory in advance of later favorable price changes.

Figure 3.2   Exchange rate returns for accumulating interbank trades

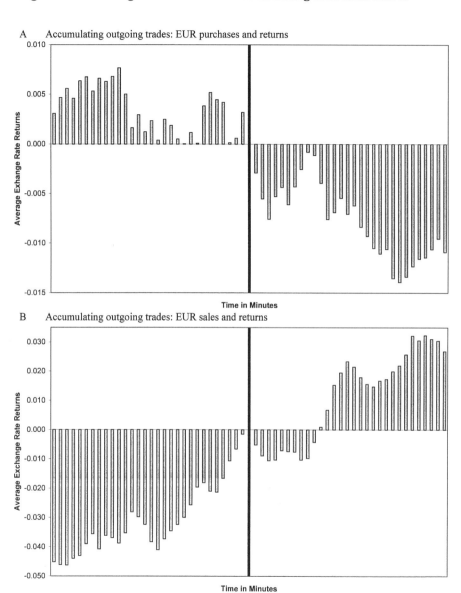

A   Accumulating outgoing trades: EUR purchases and returns

B   Accumulating outgoing trades: EUR sales and returns

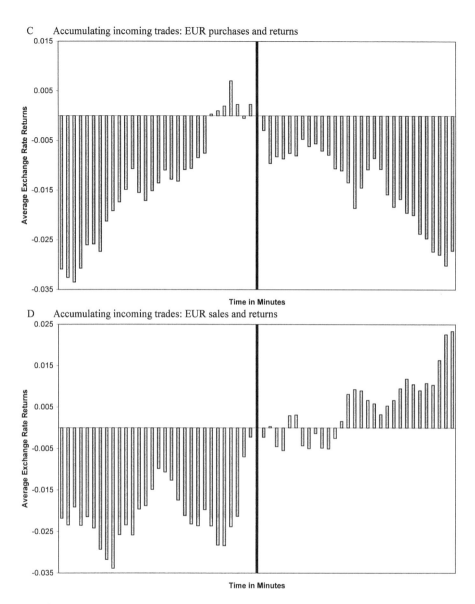

C   Accumulating incoming trades: EUR purchases and returns

D   Accumulating incoming trades: EUR sales and returns

Plot shows the developments of exchange rate returns 30 minutes before and 30 minutes after accumulating inter-bank trades. Panels A and C show returns for EUR purchases performed by outgoing trades, incoming respectively. Panels B and D show returns for EUR sales transacted via outgoing trades, incoming respectively. Accumulating interbank trades are interdealer trades of EUR 1 million and more which lead the bank's inventory away from a zero-position and which are not directly followed by an unwinding trade.

3.4.3 Revenues beyond customer trading?

A different approach to learning about speculative revenues is to estimate other revenue components which may be calculated easier. Then speculative revenues are residuals after subtracting other revenues from total. Lyons' (1998) suggestion to generally decompose the bid-ask spread cannot be justified here due to the high heterogeneity of trades. Unfortunately, Yao's (1998b) approach of calculating packages of customer plus compensating interbank trades cannot be followed either. Our bank has a much bigger share of customer trades which are partially compensating each other. Moreover, this bank does not adjust inventory shocks as fully and as quickly as Yao's bank does, possibly because the absolute size of open positions is often quite small. So, deciding about packages in Yao's sense would be highly arbitrary.

Fortunately, there may be another approach to roughly estimate revenues from non-speculative trades. For this purpose we rely on the workhorse model in FX microstructure work, i.e. the Lyons (1995) variant of Madhavan and Smidt (1991). According to this model pricing decisions on incoming orders will be influenced, among other things, by three interesting effects: first, an asset's own inventory (I) will influence price setting towards a mean-reversion of the inventory, in short the inventory effect. Second, dealers acknowledge asymmetric information among market participants in the sense that they assume private information when they set prices for a larger potential deal. They protect themselves against this assumed information disadvantage by setting larger spreads for larger orders (order size Q); in short, the information effect. Finally, traders live from buying low and selling high, so that a spread (D) is to be expected. In a companion paper, Mende, Menkhoff and Osler (2004) have extended this model to consider the three main origins of incoming trades here, i.e. interbank, financial and commercial customers' orders. This approach thus gives spreads for each group, allowing identification of possible revenues from customer trading. Taking these spreads and multiplying them by respective volumes leads to the result shown in Table 3.3 in more detail. The addition of spread-generated revenues for three counterparties leads to a total revenue of 1,435 thd. EUR (see Panel A) and thus 49% more than the true revenues of 966 thd. EUR (see Section 3.3). The shortcoming of this calculation is, however, that it overestimates revenues, as each trade receives equal weight. In fact, however, large trades will have smaller spreads than the average trade but a higher proportion in volume.

Revenues have been calculated by multiplying the absolute value of an actual trade with the estimated baseline spreads in Mende, Menkhoff and Osler (2004) (see Annex 3.1) accounting for counterparty groups only (see Panel A) and accounting for counterparty groups and trade size categories respectively (see Panel B). Absolute values of statistically significant lagged direction variable coefficients, the correctly signed coefficient for medium-sized financial customer trades have been used as well as incoming non-accumulating interbank trades have been used for revenue calculations only.

Table 3.3   Estimating revenues from customer business

EUR	Incoming, non-speculative interbank	Financial customers	Commercial customers	Total
Trading volume (millions)	1,091	405	1,181	4,122
Panel A				
Estimated spread (basis points)	1.52	2.11	10.03	
Estimated revenue accounting for counterparty groups only	165,575	85,661	1,184,189	1,435,425
Panel B				
Estimated spread (basis points)	1.28, 2.88	0, 0.77, 5.46	2.95, 8.41, 11.45	
Estimated revenue accounting for counterparty groups and trade size categories	150,525	8,647	478,516	637,688
Panel C				
Average revenue (per cent)	158,050 15	47,154 5	831,353 80	1,036,557 100

Thus, it seems advisable to disaggregate data even further and to distinguish within in each counterparty-group among trade sizes. Relying again on the coefficients found in Mende, Menkhoff and Osler (2004), there emerges a different picture. One can see, indeed, that larger trades receive smaller spreads and as these trades are more important due to their high volume, the disaggregation reduces the revenues calculated (see Table 3.3, Panel B). Without going too much into detail, the now calculated 638 thd. EUR underestimates "true" revenue as there is another significant order size component for commercial customers to be considered which increases effective spreads.

The overestimation of revenues as well as the underestimation in Table 3.3 gives a calculated band of between EUR 0.6 and 1.4 million into which the "true" revenue from interbank and customer trading will fall. For the purpose of further calculations we thus take the mean of this band-width given in Panel C. This indicates that revenues generated by position taking will be rather small, if positive at all.

3.4.4 Revenues due to price volatility?

Another strong statement helping to identify speculative revenues is from Lyons (1998, p.106): "Of course, if profits derive primarily from speculative positions, then volatility is more important than volume". It seems thus justified to analyze for our case, first, the relations between volatility and revenues and, second, the relative importance of volatility versus trading volume.

Price volatility during the day is a prerequisite for earning money from position taking. However, revenues are so small compared to volumes that tiny price changes would already be theoretically large enough to make considerable surplus. Despite this theoretical possibility, it seems plausible that larger volatility provides even better opportunities for able speculators. As a first approach to test this hypothesis for our dealer, a simple rank correlation is run between daily revenues and daily realized exchange rate volatility. Realized volatility is thereby calculated for the market from the minute-by-minute midpoint quotes which are again taken from the Olsen data base (see Section 4.3). Table 3.4 Panel A shows, however, that volatility does not seem to be significantly related to revenues.

In a second approach, we directly test Lyons' comparative statement indicating that volatility may grasp position taking, whereas volume may represent various kinds of business, such as handling incoming orders. The inclusion of trading volume can also be understood as a control variable, as the influence from volatility on revenues might be compensated by negatively related revenues from other sources, such as customer trading. The result from the baseline regression in Table 3.4, Panel B is very clear how these competing sources of revenues matter for our case: it is only volume that is significantly influential and this result holds for modifications of the baseline regression as well, such as splitting the sample, using different volatility measures or applying several kinds of volumes (not reported here).

In summary, our comparatively long time period of 87 days allows us to test for a systematic influence of daily volatility on daily revenues. There can no relation be found, indicating – in the sense of Lyons (1998) – that position taking does generate revenues for our bank via exploiting price volatility.

Table 3.4   Relations between daily revenues, exchange rate volatility and trading volume

Panel A Revenues and exchange rate (ER) volatility			
Dependent Variable: Trading revenues in EUR thousands			
Variable	Coefficient	Std. Error	t-Statistic
Constant	-0.187	7.46	-0.03
Square root of realized ER volatility (basis points)	0.204	0.12	1.64
Adjusted R^2	0.02		
Durbin-Watson stat	1.88		
Number of observations	87		

Panel B Revenues, volatility and trading volume			
Dependent Variable: Trading revenues in EUR thousands			
Variable	Coefficient	Std. Error	t-Statistic
Constant	-2.677	6.96	-0.38
Square root of realized ER volatility (basis points)	0.074	0.13	0.55
Trading volume in EUR millions	***0.204	0.04	4.89
Adjusted R^2	0.26		
Durbin-Watson stat	2.10		
Number of observations	87		

Dependent variable is daily trading revenues measured in EUR thousands. Realized exchange rate volatility is calculated by summing up squared exchange rate returns minute by minute for a each day using the Olsen data base. Trading volume is the overall daily trading volume of the bank measured in EUR millions. Estimation uses ordinary least squares with a Newey-West HAC standard errors and covariance controlling for heteroscedasticity. Standard errors and t-values are reported in the 3rd and 4th column, and "***", "**" and "*" indicate significance at the 1%, 5% and 10%-level respectively.

3.4.5 Correlates of daily revenues

This section extends the approach chosen above of explaining daily revenues more systematically. In a first step, all variables considered so far are correlated with each other, shown in Table 3.5. The matrix reveals that many variables are highly positively correlated with each other, which can make multivariate analyses problematic. In particular inventory is related to aggregated and disaggregated trading volumes, which arises naturally from the fact that any trade causes an inventory, possibly only of extremely short time. Therefore, it would be misleading to take inventory as a proxy for speculative activity. A better approach is to rely on those activities that are almost surely of speculative nature, i.e. the accumulating trades.

Table 3.5   Correlations between daily revenues and relevant variables

	Trading revenues	Total	Accumulating interbank trades	Incoming interbank trades	Outgoing interbank trades	Financial customers	Commercial customers	Realized exchange rate volatility	Average absolute inventory position
Trading revenues	1.00								
Total	0.52	1.00							
Accumulating interbank trades	0.24	0.51	1.00						
Incoming interbank trades	0.37	0.61	0.47	1.00					
Outgoing interbank trades	0.43	0.69	0.26	0.47	1.00				
Financial customers	0.35	0.38	0.17	0.23	0.15	1.00			
Commercial customers	0.34	0.83	0.17	0.25	0.49	-0.04	1.00		
Realized exchange rate volatility	0.18	0.25	0.66	0.28	0.13	0.06	0.01	1.00	
Average absolute inventory position	0.52	0.49	0.48	0.40	0.40	0.38	0.20	0.36	1.00

Putting the variables from Table 3.5 into univariate regressions explaining revenue for 87 trading days shows that volume and inventory have clear explanatory power, but that the other variables, such as price trend and price volatility, do not (not reported here). Testing several multivariate regressions always

75

leads to a similar finding: volumes are significant but indicators for speculative activity are not (see Table 3.6). Disaggregating volume according to the three main counterparty-groups shows that commercial customers are first in explaining daily revenues and financial customers second, whereas a positive revenue effect from interbank trading (being of speculative nature or not) is questionable.

These results point consistently towards a negligible role of speculation and an important role of customer business for the FX trading revenues of our bank. The next step is to go from revenue calculations to profits and to breakdown profit sources.

Table 3.6   Determinants of daily revenues

Dependent Variable: Daily trading revenues in EUR thousands			
Variable	Coefficient	Std. Error	t-Statistic
Constant	-2.036	3.09	-0.66
Accumulating interbank trading volume in EUR millions	-0.087	0.32	-0.27
Incoming interbank trading volume in EUR millions	0.275	0.23	1.19
Outgoing interbank trading volume in EUR millions	0.506	0.42	1.19
Financial customer trading volume in EUR millions	***0.410	0.08	4.87
Commercial customer trading volume in EUR millions	***0.128	0.05	2.55
Realized ER volatility (in pips)	9.246	12.37	0.75
Adjusted R^2	0.27		
Durbin-Watson stat	2.15		
Number of observations	87		

The dependent variable is daily trading revenues measured in EUR thousands. Daily interbank trading volume is split up into accumulating, incoming and outgoing trading volumes measured in EUR millions. Daily customer trading volume is divided into commercial customers and financial customers trading volume also measured in EUR millions. The realized exchange rate volatility is calculated by summing up squared exchange rate returns every minute for a whole day using the Olsen data set. Estimation uses ordinary least squares with a Newey-West HAC standard errors and covariance controlling for heteroscedasticity. Standard errors and t-values are reported in the 3rd and 4th column, and "***", "**" and "*" indicate significance at the 1%, 5% and 10%-level respectively.

3.5 Profits from different sources

3.5.1 Profits from speculation, interbank and customer trading

The first break-down of profit sources that seems interesting is between speculation and non-speculation. For this purpose the analyses conducted above to identify revenues from speculation have to be pinned down to a certain number. As no single analysis in Section 3.4 was able to identify revenues from position taking, it seems fair to conclude that these revenues should be assumed as zero.

Then costs have to be allocated. We stick here to the most restrictive concept that is to regard only those trades as speculative which can be well identified: accumulating trades. Their number amounts to 462, meaning that losses from speculation will be about 46 thd. EUR, depending on fixed costs per transaction of 100 EUR.

The next step is to decompose the non-speculating activities. They consist mainly of customer-related trading and trading in the interbank market. Both of them are intermediating activities, either between customers and the market or between banks. Following the revenue figures from Table 3.3 (Panel C) above, the estimated revenue from incoming interbank trading is 158 thd. EUR and for customer trading it is about 878 thd. EUR. What is missing so far is the fact that our bank squares many incoming orders by placing an outgoing interbank trade (Mende, Menkhoff and Osler, 2004). It seems plausible that inventory control is more important for these trades than trying to generate additional revenues. In order to learn about the disadvantage in pricing that has to be accepted to control inventory, we have added the outgoing interbank trades to the disaggregated pricing regression underlying Table 3.3. It is found that, indeed, the spread component of outgoing interbank trades is calculated as minus 1.1 basis points. These spread costs of closing incoming positions are allocated proportionally to volume as well as their fixed transaction costs. The structure of calculation and the result on profits can be seen from Table 3.7.

It is found that trading in the interbank market is only slightly profitable for our bank, a finding largely consistent with Yao (1998b, Table 7). As speculation rather leads to losses than profits, overall profitability of this bank is basically due to customer trading. This raises the question of which customer group, financial or commercial, is more profitable?

Table 3.7   Profits from speculation, other interbank and customer trading

EUR	Interbank trading			Customer trading	Total
	Speculative interbank trades [1]	Remaining interbank – incoming trades [2]	Remaining interbank – outgoing trades [2]		
Number of trades	462	992	422	1,663	3,539
Trading volume (millions)	785	1,091	659	1,586	4,122
Estimated revenues [3]	0	158,050	-103,359	878,507	933,197
Adjusted revenues [4]	0	163,654	-107,024	909,660	966,290
Direct costs [5]	46,200	99,200	42,200	166,300	353,900
Indirect costs [6]		60,831		88,394	149,224
Profit [7]	-46,200	3,624		654,966	612,390
Profit per trade	-100	4		394	173
Profit margin	-0.59	0.03		4.13	1.49

[1] Accumulating trades of EUR 1 million and more that increase inventory without being followed by an unwinding trade.
[2] Interbank trades that are not classified as speculative.
[3] The revenue figures are taken from Table 3 Panel C.
[4] Revenues are adjusted to the actual overall trading revenue of EUR 966,290 (see Table 3.2).
[5] Fixed trading costs are set to EUR 100.
[6] Non-speculative interbank outgoing trades basically serve to control inventory. They are indirect costs of incoming orders. Their negative revenue of EUR 107 thd. as well as their direct costs of EUR 42 thd. are treated as indirect costs of EUR 149 thd. These indirect costs are allocated on (remaining) incoming interbank trades and customer trades according to volume of these trades.
[7] Profit is calculated as adjusted revenue minus direct costs and minus indirect costs due to outgoing interbank trades controlling inventory.

3.5.2 Profits from financial and commercial customers

The decomposition of customer business into these two groups has been performed before by Yao (1998b, Table 6) only, on the basis of 141 financial and 53 commercial customer orders. Moreover, these trades are quite large with average volumes of 32 and 15 mill. USD respectively (p.22). Due to the larger volumes of financial institutions, the profit per trade for this group is 1,800 USD and thus clearly higher than for commercial customers with 1,200 USD despite a profit margin of 0.57 basis points only, compared to 0.78 for commercial customers. Yao concludes that there are no major differences between both groups. It is known from the spreads given in Table 3.3 above that this is not the case here. Instead, spreads at our bank are considerably smaller for financial customers, which may influence profitability. Applying the same kind of calculations as before leads to the result that commercial customers are more profitable than financial customers in all dimensions (see Table 3.8, Panel A): total profits are higher, the profit margin is higher and even profits per deal are a bit better.

3.5.3 Profits from small, medium and large customers

In a last analysis, the figures for financial and commercial customers are further decomposed into small, medium and large customers. The distinction into these three groups has been made according to the view of FX dealers: "large" are those trades that reach the minimum size of the electronic brokerage system, i.e. 1 mill. EUR or more. "Small" are trades below 0.5 mill. EUR where the bank may not adjust its inventory position and "medium" is the remaining range between 0.5 and 1 mill. EUR. Again using the above developed framework to calculate revenues and profits, the result is given in Panel B of Table 3.8. One can immediately recognize consider-able differences between customers of different size. In detail, there are six groups to be differentiated.

The most profitable in absolute terms (442 thd. EUR) as well as in terms of profit per trade (3,401 EUR) are large commercial customer trades. These trades make up about 24% of total trading volume, 53% of total revenues and even 72% of total profits. The second most important, generating another 28% of profits, are small commercial customers. This is the only group where profits per trade are so small – about 133 EUR – that higher administrative costs than the assumed 100 EUR would significantly influence their contribution. The profit contribution of the remaining four groups is between minus 29 thd. and plus 44 thd. EUR and thus not decisive for the overall profit situation of this bank's FX dealing.

What may be somewhat surprising is the finding for large financial customers. This group is the second most important in terms of trade volume but their spread is about zero. Why does the bank trade so heavily with large financial customers when it does not make money and why is the spread for this group so much smaller than for the large commercial customers? Possible explanations center around information asymmetries: first, the difference between both groups – financial and commercial customers – may reflect market power, possibly due to different investment in in-formation by customers. Second, the difference may reflect the information that the bank receives when dealing with these groups. In this sense, commercial customer flows show no relation with exchange rate changes, whereas financial customer flows are highly correlated with market price changes and in this sense informative (Fan and Lyons, 2003; Mende, Menkhoff and Osler, 2004).

Table 3.8   Profits from financial and commercial customers

PANEL A Customer groups	All cus- tomer trades	Financial cus- tomer trades	Commercial cus- tomer trades
Number of trades	1,663	171	1,492
Trading volume (millions)	1,586	405	1,181
Estimated revenue	1,269,851	85,661	1,184,189
Adjusted revenue [1]	909,660	61,364	848,296
Direct costs [2]	166,300	17,100	149,200
Indirect costs [3]	88,394	22,572	65,822
Profit	654,966	21,692	633,275
Profit per trade	394	127	424
Profit margin	4.13	0.54	5.36

PANEL B Customers groups according to trade size	Financial customer trades			Commercial customer trades		
	Large	Me-dium	Small	Large	Me-dium	Small
Number of trades	77	24	70	130	81	1,281
Trading volume (millions)	375	17	13	976	54	151
Estimated revenue	0	1,307	7,340	287,446	17,775	173,295
percent	0	15	85	60	4	36
Adjusted revenue [1]	0	9,276	52,087	509,574	31,511	307,211
Direct costs [2]	7,700	2,400	7,000	13,000	8,100	128,100
Indirect costs [3]	20,900	947	725	54,396	3,010	8,416
Profit	-28,600	5,929	44,363	442,178	20,402	170,695
Profit per trade	-371	247	634	3,401	252	133
Profit margin	-0.76	3.49	34.13	4.53	3.78	11.30

[1] Revenues are adjusted to the overall customer trading revenue of EUR 909,660.
[2] Fixed trading costs are set to EUR 100.
[3] Indirect costs are costs of non-speculative interbank outgoing trades that are allocated according to volume.

3.6 Conclusions

This analysis of the trading record of a small bank has revealed new findings about profits and profit sources in FX trading. First of all, we find that our small bank, indeed, generates considerable revenues as well as profits from its FX trading operations. It is difficult to assess from outside how satisfying profitability is regarded for the overall bank but considerable profits are real. The degree of profitability is in between the two other cases of large banks documented before (Lyons, 1998; Yao, 1998b). Second, speculative position taking by the bank cannot be identified as profitable. This is somewhat surprising, as earlier studies indicated a range of 0 to 30% profit share for speculative trading. Third, this is the first study to disaggregate overall revenues and profits into customer groups. It is found that only one group is decisive for profitability, i.e. large commercial customers. Again, this may be surprising as Braas and Bralver (1990) suppose that smaller banks make money only with small customers, but this contradiction could be caused by different views on size: large in our case means a trade size of one million Euro and more, the median being at 3.05 million Euro – seen for example from Yao's bank, these trades are clearly below average.

Particular attention has been paid to detecting revenues from speculation where we can apply new approaches due to the detailed and long sample. An event study approach has been applied to follow prices after the bank had become engaged in accumulating trades: there is no indication that revenues are earned. Seen from the opposite side, i.e. from customer business, the latter can explain all revenues earned and there is no room for speculative profits. In another attempt, profits have been related to volatility in the foreign exchange market but our bank does not seem to take advantage of volatile markets. Finally, the several profit sources have been put in a multivariate approach, which confirms findings: as neither speculation nor interbank trading contributes much to revenues, it is only customer business that is significantly related to profits.

The other major concern in this study has been the disaggregation of profits in customer trading. We present evidence that financial customers are much less attractive in this respect than commercial customers. Five of the six groups distinguished are profitable, so it is particularly interesting that large financial customers do not contribute at all. By contrast, the large commercial customers are the main profit source.

The common ground for these findings may be based in the informative situation of the small bank. This bank acts as a marginal market maker, i.e. it is active to some degree in the interbank market but it is too small to emulate the big ones. So it is extremely difficult for this dealer to gain any informative advantage against the leading FX trading banks. The same applies in comparison to big institutional investors. The bank has a better position, however, in relation to its commercial customers. The latter obviously do not care too much about a spread of 5 or 10 basis points, depending on size. These small spreads are enough for our bank to unload positions, to manage its overall inventory and to cover administrative costs. This successful service makes clear, moreover, that the small bank – possibly other small participants too – is not engaged in stabilizing speculation in Friedman's sense. It rather acts as price-taker in a huge market where risk is allocated and information traded.

Annex 3.1 Estimation of Lyons' (1995) baseline model for all incoming trades

Panel A   Modified baseline model for different counterparty groups

Results for all incoming trades	Coefficient	Standard error
Constant	**-0.522	0.23
Order flow		
Interbank	-0.206	0.40
Financial customer	1.179	1.08
Commercial customer	0.679	0.44
Inventory		
Interbank trades	-0.270	0.35
Lagged	0.175	0.35
Financial customer trades	1.297	1.06
Lagged	-1.422	1.07
Commercial customer trades	**1.000	0.43
Lagged	**-1.079	0.43
Direction		
Interbank trades, current	***2.952	0.69
Lagged	***-1.517	0.48
Financial customer trades, current	***5.171	1.46
Lagged	*-2.114	1.17
Commercial customer trades, current	***11.906	0.52
Lagged	***-10.027	0.49
Adjusted R^2		0.23
Number of observations		2,859

The dependent variable is Δp_t, the change in price between two successive trades measured in pips. Q_t is order flow measured in EUR millions multiplied with a dummy variable for each counterparty group, i.e. other dealers, commercial or financial customers respectively. I_t is the dealer's inventory at time t multiplied with a dummy variable for each counterparty group. D_t is an indicator variable picking up the direction of the trade, positive for purchases (at the ask) and negative for sales (at the bid) again multiplied with a dummy variable for each counterparty group and dummy variables accounting for trade size categories respectively in Panel B. Estimation uses GMM and Newey-West correction. Standard errors in the third column, and "***", "**" and "*" indicate significance at the 1%, 5% and 10%-level respectively.

Annex 3.1 Estimation of Lyons' (1995) baseline model for all incoming trades (continued)

Panel B   Extended hierarchy baseline model and different counterparty groups

Results for all incoming trades	Coefficient	Standard error
Constant	-0.257	0.22
Order flow		
Interbank	-0.448	0.39
Financial customer	1.085	0.98
Commercial customer	**0.916	0.46
Inventory		
Interbank	-0.223	0.36
Lagged	0.163	0.36
Financial customer trades	0.996	0.96
Lagged	-1.135	0.96
Commercial customer trades	**0.993	0.41
Lagged	**-1.013	0.41
Direction		
Interbank trades, large	***3.869	0.74
Lagged	***-1.282	0.51
Interbank trades, small	1.429	1.22
Lagged	***-2.883	1.33
Financial customer trades, large	1.208	1.94
Lagged	0.509	1.81
Financial customer trades, medium	3.610	2.46
Lagged	-0.772	2.39
Financial customer trades, small	***9.247	2.49
Lagged	***-5.461	1.67
Commercial customer trades, large	***4.142	1.73
Lagged	***-2.947	1.27
Commercial customer trades, medium	***14.043	1.59
Lagged	***-8.410	1.64
Commercial customer trades, small	***12.811	0.57
Lagged	***-11.447	0.57
Adjusted R^2		0.24
Number of observations		2,859

The dependent variable is Δp_t, the change in price between two successive trades measured in pips. Q_t is order flow measured in EUR millions multiplied with a dummy variable for each counterparty group, i.e. other dealers, commercial or financial customers respectively. I_t is the dealer's inventory at time t multiplied with a dummy variable for each counterparty group. D_t is an indicator variable picking up the direction of the trade, positive for purchases (at the ask) and negative for sales (at the bid) again multiplied with a dummy variable for each counterparty group and dummy variables accounting for trade size categories respectively in Panel B. Estimation uses GMM and Newey-West correction. Standard errors in the third column, and "***", "**" and "*" indicate significance at the 1%, 5% and 10%-level respectively.

4   September 11th on the Foreign Exchange Market[*]

4.1   Introduction

On September 11th 2001 the United States experienced its most devastating terrorist attack when terrorists crashed hijacked airliners into the World Trade Center and the Pentagon. The tragic events affected not only people all over the world, but also the financial markets worldwide. Because of the attacks and damage to the New York City financial district, US financial markets were closed until September 17th (see Carter and Simkins, 2002). When the markets opened again stock prices were exposed to substantial turbulences. Airline and tourist industry stock prices fell rapidly. Stock markets in Europe were more vulnerable to US stock market shocks even months after the tragedy (see Carter and Simkins, 2002; Hon, Strauss and Yong, 2004).

The question arises as to how foreign exchange markets reacted, in particular the USD/EUR market. Did the events of September 11th have any influence on the exchange rate or the determinants of foreign exchange trading? Did the USD/EUR market suffer a liquidity squeeze? The general notion seems to be that foreign exchange markets simply absorbed any kind of shock due to the quick response of central bank authorities (providing liquidity) and due to the decentralized structure of the markets themselves (see for example Bishop, 2002). However, empirical evidence in support of this view has not yet been available.

This paper provides answers to these questions. We are looking at the relationships between trading volume, volatility and spreads, which provide insights into the structure of foreign exchange markets. The issue is important because of its implications for the analysis of market liquidity and exchange rate risk. The empirical microstructure literature has typically found a positive correlation between trading volumes, volatility and spreads in financial markets (see Karpoff, 1987). But especially in times of stress these relations can change dramatically, indicating high or low market liquidity respectively (see Sarr and Lybek, 2002; Galati, 2003).

In particular, we study the relationship between foreign exchange trading activities, realized exchange rate volatility and bid-ask spreads on the USD/EUR foreign exchange market on the basis of a unique joint data set, consisting of actual transaction data of a small bank in Germany and market-wide quoted data. We also glance at the GBP/EUR and the CHF/EUR markets for comparative reasons. We focus on the volume-volatility-spread-relation because it depends not only on the market-size and its degree of liquidity, but also on the rate

---

*   I would like to thank Lukas Menkhoff, Michael Frömmel, Rafael Rebitzki, Daniela Beckmann, Torben Lütje and Josefin Cejie for helpful comments.

of information flow to the market (Karpoff, 1987). Knowledge of these relations can be used to measure changes of the price process due to a sudden event. To our knowledge there is no other study existent which examines these relationships around September 11th on the basis of both market-wide data and so-called tick-by-tick trading data, and thus, analyzing real trading behavior and quoting activity at the same time.

We find that for USD/EUR, GBP/EUR and CHF/EUR realized volatility and quoted spreads are by far larger during the events of September 11th than before. The shock is not persistent though and the impact on volatilities and spreads already vanishes after approximately one to three days. As expected, we find a positive correlation between trading activity and volatility. This relationship does not break up during the events, as a Chow Breakpoint Test confirms. Quite the contrary, the relationship intensifies strongly during the incidents of September 11th, indicating the massive arrival of new information, uncertainty and increased exchange rate risk. The foreign exchange market maintains its very liquid structure and its efficient processing of exogenous shocks. In accordance with Bjønnes, Rime and Solheim (2003), we also find some evidence that it is commercial customers who provide liquidity. We conclude that the main foreign exchange markets – especially the USD/EUR market – are liquid markets due to the huge number of market participants. Their decentralized structure can be considered as a guarantor of market efficiency.

The remainder proceeds as follows. Section 4.2 introduces the joint data set we use. In Section 4.3 we first introduce the common theoretical background. We then present the results of our estimations, both on a daily basis and a 10-minute interval basis, after. Section 4.4 concludes.

4.2 Data Description

The data set used in this study is compiled by two different data sets, i.e. Olsen's quoted FX spot data and actual transaction data of a small German bank respectively. Whereas the high frequency data provided by Olsen Financial Technologies Switzerland (www.olsendata.com) is publicly available – for a small fee, the bank's transaction data is of private property and only available to the author.

The latter data set consists of the complete USD/EUR, GBP/EUR and CHF/EUR trading record of a small bank in Germany. The record covers 87 trading days, beginning on Wednesday, the 11th of July 2001, and ending on Friday, the 9th of November 2001. Compared to other microstructure data sets such as Lyons (1995), Yao (1998), and Bjønnes and Rime (2003) this is the longest observation period up to date. The data overlap September 11th roughly symmetrically.

The transaction data contain all trades, including indirect trades executed by voice-brokers or electronic brokerage systems such as EBS, direct trades completed by telephone or electronically, internal trades and customer trades.[37] All trades are entered manually into the "deals blotter" by the back-office without differentiating between the several trading channels of each transaction. Bid-offer quotes at the time of each transaction are not recorded, either, but we can easily identify bid-offer prices afterwards by means of the trade-initiating party.

For each transaction we have the exact date and time, the type of the trade, the counterparty, i.e. another bank, financial or commercial customer respectively, the amount traded, its price and some further information.[38] The variables we obtain are the daily exchange rate[39], the daily spread and – disentangled for counterparty groups – the daily number of trades, trading volumes, order imbalances and flows.

Whereas this part of the data set covers actual transactions of a single market participant, the other part of the data set consists of market-wide – yet quoted – foreign exchange data. Olsen's FX spot data records all best and last bid and ask quotes as well as the number of quotes every minute, 24 hours a day, for USD/EUR, GBP/EUR and CHF/EUR, from the beginning of July until the end of November 2001.

We have adjusted this massive amount of data in order to match our own individual trade data. Therefore we set the time period from July 11th to November 9th and only use the minute-by-minute quote data from 8:00 to 18:00 (MET) as our bank has not carried out any transaction before or after. We thus get 600 observations per day. We also obtain the quoted exchange rate, i.e. the midpoint of best bid and best ask quote, the narrowest quoted spread, i.e. the gap between best bid and best ask quote every minute, and the number of ticks, i.e. the number of quotes every minute, for each currency pair. We average out an exchange rate, i.e. average of "best midpoints", and a bid-ask spread, i.e. average of "best spreads".

---

37 In order to obtain an even broader data set, we include outright-forward trades in an adjusted manner, i.e. by correcting for the forward points. In our opinion, these trades should not be disregarded, as we also focus on customer trading, and outright-forward trades account for a large portion of customer business. Moreover, outright-forward trades influence the inventory position in our bank, as this trading is also conducted by, and accounted for, the same dealer as the spot trading.

38 For a more detailed description of this part of the data set, please refer to Mende, Menkhoff and Osler (2004). Some cases are deleted from the data due to extreme price changes of more than 100 basis points or tiny volumes of less than 1,000 USD, as both characteristics may blur the relationships of interest. We have also excluded so-called "preferred commercial customer business" since associated prices may reflect cross-selling arrangements.

39 Each day we average out the overall bid and ask rate, i.e. amount of USD sold (bought) divided by amount of EUR bought (sold). We chose the midpoint as the daily exchange rate.

The frequency of quotes is commonly used as a proxy for the overall trading activity in foreign exchange microstructure literature (see Goodhart and Figliuoli, 1991; Bollerslev and Domowitz, 1993; Melvin and Yin, 2000). To measure the intraday and daily volatility of exchange rates we decided to use the realized volatility, i.e. sum of squared changes between the logs of the exchange rate. Many papers have documented the excellent performance of the realized volatility as a volatility measure and it has become common use – especially in high-frequency data analyses (see for example Frankel and Wei, 1991; Jorion, 1996; Poon, Blair and Taylor, 2001; Andersen, Bollerslev and Diebold, 2003; Andersen, Bollerslev and Meddahi, 2003, Galati, 2003; Koopman, Jungbacken and Hol, 2004). In our case it also provides the best empirical results compared to other measures of volatility.[40]

In order to establish a link between market-wide foreign exchange activity during the turbulences of the September 11th events and the actual trading activity of our particular market participant during that time, we need to merge both data sets. We bring the two data sets together on a daily basis and on a basis of a time-interval of 10 minutes.[41] The latter part of the merged data set only covers the days 10th, 11th and 12th of September 2001. But is it justified to actually assume that real transaction data of a small, almost marginal, market participant somewhat mirrors the market-wide quoted data? This is why we check whether prices of the actual transacted deals behave in any way differently from the quoted ones. Figure 4.1 represents the movements of the quoted exchange rates, i.e. the midpoints of best bid and ask quotes every minute averaged out each day, and the calculated midpoints of daily volume-weighted prices of actual foreign exchange trades of the small German bank. Obviously calculated prices and quoted exchange rates are almost identical for USD/EUR, GBP/EUR and CHF/EUR. Thus, the bank's foreign exchange trading is in tune with worldwide market developments.

---

40 We have tried other measures of volatility, too, such as the standard deviations and volatilities generated by a GARCH (1,1) process.

41 We have tried other time intervals, too, but either there are not enough observations within a chosen interval regarding the small bank's transaction data, or there are not enough observations during a single trading day if we choose a larger interval.

Figure 4.1   Quoted exchange rates and calculated FX prices

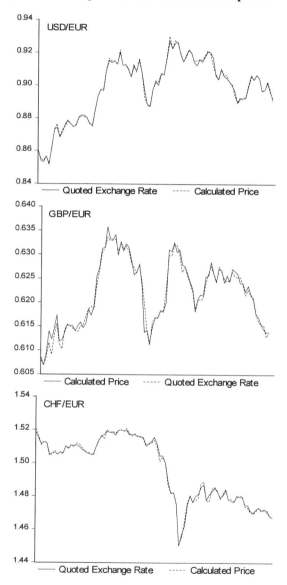

Figure shows quoted USD/EUR, GBP/EUR and CHF/EUR exchange rates taken from the Olsen data set, and the corresponding calculated foreign exchange prices, taken from the small bank's trading record over the whole sample period (07/11/01 – 11/09/01).

To measure market-wide trading activity the bank's overall number of trades in USD/EUR seems to be a good proxy as we find a cointegration relation between number of trades and number of ticks (not reported here).[42] We merge market-wide quoted data and the small bank's trading data for USD/EUR trading as the USD/EUR foreign exchange market was possibly in the midst of the events. We use daily data of GBP/EUR and CHF/EUR for comparative reasons. Variables of interest are: number of trades, trading volume and absolute values of intraday order imbalances for different counterparty groups. Table 4.1 presents statistics about these variables. Widest spreads are quoted in the CHF/EUR market, tightest in the GBP/EUR market although they are all between moderately 2 and 5 basis points. Trading and quoting activity seems to be higher in GBP/EUR and USD/EUR market than the foreign exchange trading in CHF/EUR. You can also see that the small bank trades remarkably less in GBP/EUR and CHF/EUR than in USD/EUR. Realized volatility is lowest in the CHF/EUR market. Maximum values of spreads and volatilities are always realized on September 11th while the other variables do not reach a peak on that very day.

Table 4.2 shows correlations between various important daily variables for USD/EUR. Realized exchange rate volatility, spreads and number of ticks (and trades) reveal the strongest positive correlation with each other. There is a high impact of the dummy-variable "September 11th" on those variables, too, and alleviated even on the absolute value of customer order imbalances. The weak – but yet positive – correlations between number of trades and the trading activity variables at the small bank on the one hand and the weak – but yet positive – correlation between number of trades and realized volatility and spreads on the other, indicate the connection between individual trading determinants and market wide activity. Again, quoted and calculated exchange rates show that they are nearly identical with a positive correlation of one.

---

42 The bank's overall number of trades in GBP/EUR and CHF/EUR trading cannot be used in the same way because there are way too few transactions in this part of the bank's foreign exchange trading. The number of ticks provided by Olsen is not fully reliable when summed up on a daily basis due to accidental double counting at times between August 14th and September 12th for USD/EUR. Therefore we will not make use of this variable in our analyses on a daily basis. The bank's daily trading volume measured in EUR millions is not a good proxy for market-wide trading activities, either. Its daily turnover of roughly EUR 61 millions (USD/EUR, GBP/EUR and CHF/EUR altogether) is tiny compared to overall daily turnover of approximately USD 390 billions (USD/EUR, GBP/EUR and CHF/EUR in sum) (see BIS, 2002).

Table 4.1   Descriptive statistics on a daily basis

Table shows descriptive statistics of daily USD/EUR, GBP/EUR and CHF/EUR trading activity determinants of a small bank in Germany over the 87 trading days between July 11th, 2001, and November 9th, 2001, i.e. numbers of trades, absolute values of customer order imbalances, overall and customer trading volumes. It also shows statistics on the corresponding market-wide determinants generated from the quoted Olsen data, i.e. spread, realized volatility and number of ticks.

A   Survey of USD/EUR data

USD/EUR	Spread (pips)	Realized volatility	Number of trades	Number of ticks	Absolute value of customer order imbalances (millions)	Overall trading volume (millions)	Customer trading volume (millions)
Mean	2.40	0.3230	41	16,504	5.504	42.679	16.323
Median	2.34	0.2800	39	14,216	1.757	33.789	9.065
Maximum	4.62	1.8000	129	35,290	45.478	212.224	157.798
Minimum	1.73	0.1540	13	8,947	0.024	6.724	0.604
September 11th	4.62	1.8000	63	31,694	37.981	118.888	38.502
Std. Dev.	0.46	0.1970	17.43	6,558	8.426	33.440	23.870
Observations	87	87	87	87	87	87	87

B   Survey of GBP/EUR data

GBP/EUR	Spread (pips)	Realized volatility	Number of trades	Number of ticks	Absolute value of customer order imbalances (millions)	Overall trading volume (millions)	Customer trading volume (millions)
Mean	1.93	0.3420	7	10,270	2.009	7.793	5.333
Median	1.93	0.3130	6	11,136	0.104	2.585	0.534
Maximum	3.27	1.3700	27	19,414	42.971	43.616	42.978
Minimum	1.30	0.2180	1	3,751	0	0.001	0.000
September 11th	3.27	1.3700	6	14,806	0.185	0.989	0.185
Std. Dev.	0.34	0.1450	4.13	4,343	5.851	10.748	9.823
Observations	87	87	87	87	87	87	87

C   Survey of CHF/EUR data

CHF/EUR	Spread (pips)	Realized volatility	Number of trades	Number of ticks	Absolute value of customer order imbalances (millions)	Overall trading volume (millions)	Customer trading volume (millions)
Mean	4.87	0.2299	6	11,164	1.507	10.876	3.458
Median	5.04	0.2043	5	12,094	0.090	5.524	0.436
Maximum	8.47	0.8148	32	20,038	25.629	59.786	42.224
Minimum	2.67	0.1272	1	3,205	0.000	0.004	0.000
September 11th	8.47	0.8148	4	16,119	0.000	4.535	0.000
Std. Dev.	1.34	0.1008	4.45	5,540	3.896	13.025	7.167
Observations	87	87	87	87	87	87	87

Table 4.2   Correlations of variables for USD/EUR

USD/EUR	Spread	Realized volatility	Number of ticks	Number of trades	Trading volume	Volume of customer trades	Volume of incoming interbank trades	Absolute value of customer order imbalances	September 11th	Calculated exchange rate	Quoted exchange rate
Spread	1.00										
Realized volatility	0.80	1.00									
Number of ticks	0.71	0.43	1.00								
Number of trades	0.41	0.34	0.39	1.00							
Trading volume	0.19	0.25	0.20	0.48	1.00						
Volume of customer trades	0.01	0.04	0.02	0.27	0.91	1.00					
Volume of incoming interbank trades	0.32	0.39	0.34	0.58	0.60	0.27	1.00				
Absolute value of customer order imbalances	0.30	0.39	0.24	0.46	0.58	0.41	0.41	1.00			
September 11th	0.53	0.81	0.25	0.14	0.25	0.10	0.27	0.42	1.00		
Calculated exchange rate	0.13	0.05	0.20	0.15	-0.07	-0.11	0.08	-0.07	0.02	1.00	
Quoted exchange rate	0.12	0.04	0.20	0.15	-0.07	-0.11	0.07	-0.07	0.01	1.00	1.00

4.3 Foreign exchange trading during the events of September 11th
4.3.1 Trading volume, volatility and spreads in the literature

There is vast amount of literature examining the relationship between trading volume, volatility and spreads in financial markets with regard to measuring liquidity. Whilst Karpoff (1987) provides a detailed overview of earlier literature, Hasbrouck and Seppi (2001) and Sarr and Lybek (2002) summarize and evaluate different liquidity measures for different financial markets up to date. Lyons (2001) and Sarno and Taylor (2001) review such work on foreign exchange markets. The overall finding is a positive correlation between different measures of trading volume and price volatility on the one hand, and also a positive correlation between volume, volatility and bid-ask spreads on the other hand, which holds for different data frequencies (see for example Harris, 1986; Bollerslev and Melvin, 1994; Jorion, 1996; Chordia, Roll and Subrahmanyam, 2001; Bjønnes, Rime and Solheim, 2002; Galati, 2003).

In economic theory there are different explanations for the co-movement of trading volume and volatility of which we favor the so-called "mixture of distributions hypothesis" (MDH) which was first proposed by Clark (1973). The MDH states that volume and volatility are both driven by the same, unobservable factor – the arrival of public information – in two opposite ways (see Tauchen and Pitts, 1983). First, as the number of traders grows prices become less volatile. Second, an increase in volume reflects greater disagreement among a given number of traders about new information and hence leads to higher volatility. In a more liquid market the second link should outweigh the first, as the number of traders is already large enough to provide immediacy, i.e. a high speed of order execution, and depth, i.e. order abundance.[43]

Besides such volume-based measures of liquidity there are also liquidity measures which are based on transaction costs: bid-ask spreads.[44] In dealer markets spreads typically reflect three types of costs among others. (i) Order processing costs and (ii) asymmetric information costs to account for the possibility that the counterparty is privately informed. (iii) Inventory costs are associated with the costs of holding open positions. This third component is especially exposed to changes in volume and volatility. A positive correlation between exchange rate volatility and spreads reflects price risk. A positive correlation be-

---

[43] Other works for example were based on models of "sequential information arrival" (Copeland, 1976), according to which information reaches one market participant at a time. As that agent reacts to the arrival of news, his demand curve will shift, which leads to a positive correlation between volume and volatility.

[44] Sarr and Lybek (2002) also discuss price-based and market-impact measures as well as other econometric techniques to measure market liquidity, which we will not consider here.

tween trading volume and spreads reflects the arrival of news and hence a higher price risk.[45]

The abovementioned relationships have been confirmed by numerous empirical studies for many financial markets, using all kinds of volatility and trading volume measures. But, unlike other financial markets, most of the trading in foreign exchange markets is conducted over the counter, and therefore comprehensive high-frequency data on actual trading volume are generally not available to researchers. Thus, alternative measures for trading volume have to be pulled up. Studies using easier to obtain data on future contracts also find a positive correlation between volume and volatility (see Jorion, 1996; Wang and Yau, 2000). However, because trading volume in foreign exchange future markets is comparatively small, such studies may not reflect the behavior of total foreign exchange market activity. Other studies rely on indicative quotes by Reuters or other providers instead (see Goodhart and Figliuoli, 1991; Bollerslev and Domowitz, 1993; Goodhart, Ito and Payne, 1996; Melvin and Yin, 2000). They usually find a positive relation between quoting activity – used as a proxy for trading activity – and volatility, too. Nevertheless, quotes do not represent actual trades. So the revealed relationship might be misrepresented. Studies by Wei (1994) and Hartmann (1999) focus on YEN/USD transaction data provided by the Bank of Japan. Unfortunately, they represent not more than 5% of the global market.

A big step forward was made by looking at high-frequency data on actual transactions in the spirit of the new microstructure approach to exchange rates (Lyons, 2001). Data sets as used in Lyons (1995), Yao (1998), Bjønnes and Rime (2003), and Mende, Menkhoff and Osler (2004) cover all transactions of individual foreign exchange dealers and provide useful insights in the displayed behavior of market participants. Unfortunately, they typically map only a very limited segment of the market and mostly cover a short time period.

Two exceptions are noteworthy. Galati (2003) collects broader data for several emerging market countries. He records actual trading volume, fairly covering the total trading activity in those foreign exchange markets. He receives mixed results for different countries, though he is generally able to confirm the MDH. He finds indications that the degree of liquidity can be measured by the relation between volume, volatility and spreads and that this degree dif-

---

45 When it comes to the relationship of trading volume and bid-ask spreads, sometimes two different impacts are considered depending on whether volume is expected or unexpected. Expected trading volume should generally have a negative impact on spread sizes as it reflects economies of scales (Cornell, 1978). On the other hand, unexpected trading volume should be positively correlated with spreads because it reflects the arrival of news and hence increases price risk. For example, Hartman (1999) shows that unpredictable foreign exchange turnover increases spreads, while predictable turnover decreases them.

fers for periods "under stress", i.e. the positive relation between trading volume and volatility breaks down during turbulent times in some markets.

Bjønnes, Rime and Solheim (2002) study the SEK/DEM foreign exchange market. Their data set covers a remarkable 95% of the market revealing a positive correlation of trading volume and volatility. This relation is strongest for "foreign customers" and "other banks". These results suggest a high level of liquidity in foreign exchange markets of developed countries. They also indicate that heterogeneity matters for foreign exchange trading – by now a general finding also confirmed by Fan and Lyons (2003), and Mende, Menkhoff and Osler (2004).

By combining our two data sets we are able to connect actual trades to market-wide foreign exchange prices and hence measure real trading activity and market developments applied to one of the main foreign exchange markets.

4.3.2 Impact and persistence of September 11th on daily trading determinants

Figure 4.2A-E provides a general overview of the behavior of daily trading determinants during the observation period. Figure 4.2A again plots the quoted and calculated USD/EUR, GBP/EUR and CHF/EUR exchange rates. The vertical line represents September 11th. One can see that there were no substantial changes in the exchange rate movement. Figure 4.2B shows the realized exchange rate volatilities and Figure 4.2C quoted bid-ask spreads for all three currencies. These values stand out. Volatilities and spreads are by far larger on September 11th than before or after. Simple t-tests show that volatility and spreads after the event are not generally different from those before (not reported here). In Figure 4.2D we have plotted daily trading volume and numbers of trades transacted at our bank. Although there is a peak on September 11th for USD/EUR it is by far not the highest. Volume and trading activity for GBP/EUR and CHF/EUR are not noteworthy on September 11th. Figure 4.2E represents customer order imbalances on a daily basis, i.e. the excess demand of customers. Again, there is a peak in the USD/EUR data but not an exceptional one. There is almost no customer trading activity in GBP/EUR and CHF/EUR on that very day.

Figure 4.2A   September 11th and exchange rates

USD/EUR Exchange rate

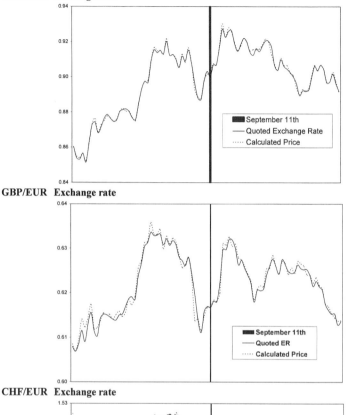

GBP/EUR Exchange rate

CHF/EUR Exchange rate

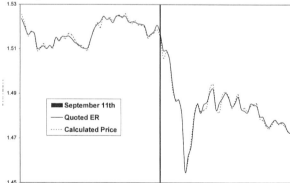

Figure shows daily USD/EUR, GBP/EUR and CHF/EUR exchange rate taken from the Olsen data set and FX prices from the small bank's trading record over the whole sample period (07/11/01 – 11/09/01). September 11th is marked with the grey vertical line.

Figure 4.2B   September 11th and realized exchange rate volatility

USD/EUR Realized exchange rate volatility

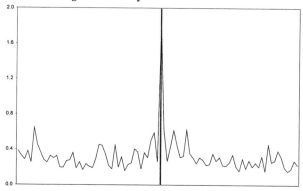

GBP/EUR Realized exchange rate volatility

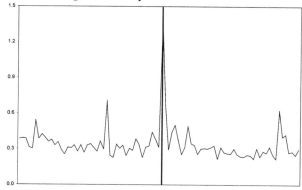

CHF/EUR Realized exchange rate volatility

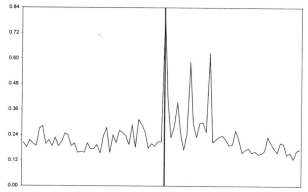

Figure shows daily USD/EUR, GBP/EUR and CHF/EUR realized exchange rate volatilities over the whole sample period (07/11/01 – 11/09/01). September 11th is marked with the grey vertical line.

Figure 4.2C   September 11th and bid-ask spreads
    USD/EUR Spread

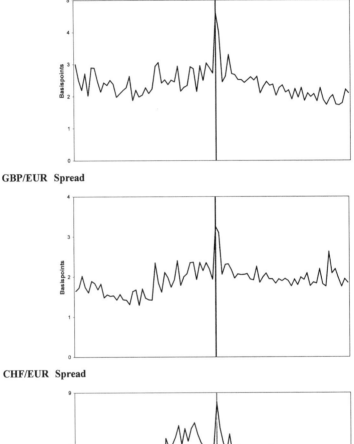

GBP/EUR Spread

CHF/EUR Spread

Figure shows USD/EUR, GBP/EUR and CHF/EUR best quoted daily bid-ask spreads measured in pips over the whole sample period (07/11/01 – 11/09/01). September 11th is marked with the grey vertical line.

Figure 4.2D   September 11th and trading activity

USD/EUR Trading activity

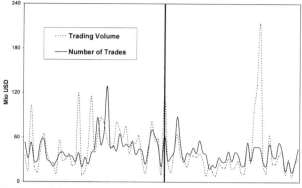

GBP/EUR Trading activity

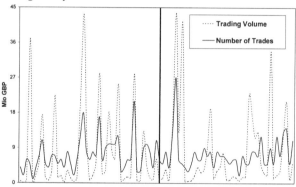

CHF/EUR Trading activity

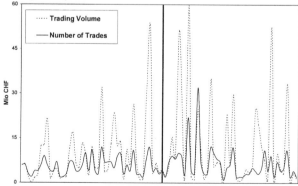

Figure shows daily USD/EUR, GBP/EUR and CHF/EUR trading volume and number of trades at small bank over the whole sample period (07/11/01 – 11/09/01). September 11th is marked with the grey vertical line.

Figure 4.2E   September 11th and customer order imbalances

USD/EUR Customer order imbalances

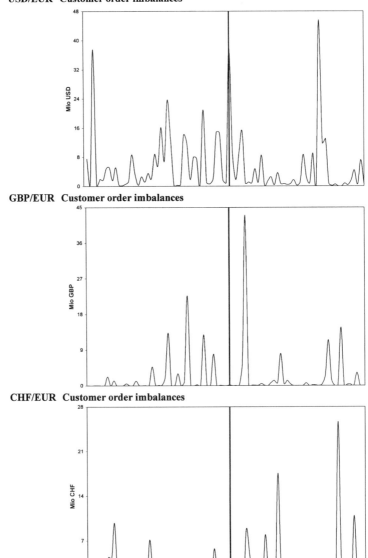

GBP/EUR Customer order imbalances

CHF/EUR Customer order imbalances

Figure shows absolute values of daily USD/EUR, GBP/EUR and CHF/EUR customer order imbalances over the whole sample period (07/11/01 – 11/09/01). September 11th is marked with the grey vertical line.

We need to generally confirm the positive relationship between volume and volatility for our joint data set between volume, volatility and spreads respectively. Therefore, we first regress realized exchange rate volatility, measured as daily sum of squared returns, on a constant and on different measures of trading volume. The results are reported in Table 4.3A.[46] The coefficient on number of trades, i.e. the daily sum of all trades of our small bank including incoming and outgoing interbank trades, commercial and financial customer trades, is positive and statistically significant. Trading volume is the bank's overall daily trading volume measured in EUR millions including all trades. The absolute value of customer order imbalances is the excess demand or supply of customer business every day also measured in EUR millions, i.e. daily customer sales and purchases that do not sum up to zero.[47] The coefficients on these two alternative measures of trading activity are positive yet statistically insignificant. Thus, number of trades seems to be an appropriate proxy for measuring trading volume. The positive correlation between trading activity and volatility is in line with the literature.[48]

Next, we analyze the relationship between bid-ask spreads, i.e. daily average of minute-by-minute gap between best quoted ask and bid, trading activity and volatility. Results are reported in Table 4.3B and C. Spreads are explained in terms of realized volatility and trading activity (Panel B) and in terms of realized volatility, expected and unexpected trading activity (Panel C).[49] Volatility and number of trades (expected and unexpected) are significantly positively correlated with the spread-size, indicating that spreads increase due to a higher price risk. These results confirm the general cognition of the volume-volatility-spread relationship in foreign exchange markets.

---

46 We have also tested for day-of-week effects (see Annex 4.1). The results show no significant influence of the weekday though.

47 Order imbalances are used in Chordia, Roll and Subrahmanyam (2002) for example in order to measure the pressure on the bank to square customer orders at the interbank market.

48 For GBP/EUR and CHF/EUR we receive similar results using number ticks instead of number of trades. In the USD/EUR data number of ticks is also positively correlated to the exchange rate volatility at a statistically significant level. These results are not reported here though, because they only represent the quoted part of the joint data set.

49 Number of trades is decomposed into an expected and an unexpected component by using an ARMA(1,1) series and its residuals according to Galati (2003). This decomposition may not be fully adaptable here, as we use the trading activity of a small bank as a proxy for trading volume which should be unpredictable for the market as a whole.

Table 4.3   Volatility, spreads and different measures of trading volume

A   Volatility and different measures of trading volume

Dependent Variable: Realized exchange rate volatility

Variable	Coefficient	t-Statistic
Constant	-0.183	-1.22
Log of number of trades	***0.129	2.55
Trading volume in EUR millions	0.000	0.17
Absolute value of customer order imbalances in EUR millions	0.006	0.83
AR(1)	***0.242	4.08
Adjusted R^2	0.19	
Observations	86	

B   Spreads and different measures of trading volume

Dependent Variable: Quoted spread

Variable	Coefficient	t-Statistic
Constant	***0.951	3.66
Realized exchange rate volatility	***1.758	12.31
Log of number of trades	***0.263	3.52
Trading volume in EUR millions	-0.001	-1.62
Absolute value of customer order imbalances in EUR millions	-0.002	-0.50
Adjusted R^2	0.65	
Observations	87	

C   Spreads, expected and unexpected trading volume

Dependent Variable: Quoted spread

Variable	Coefficient	t-Statistic
Constant	0.353	0.72
Realized exchange rate volatility	***1.724	11.43
Log of expected number of trades	***0.410	3.01
Log of unexpected number of trades	***0.404	3.05
Adjusted R^2	0.66	
Observations	86	

The dependent variable is the daily realized exchange rate volatility, daily quoted spread respectively. Number of trades is the overall number of foreign exchange deal transacted at the small German bank each day. Trading volume is the daily overall trading volume at the bank measured in EUR millions. Customer order imbalances are the daily foreign exchange excess-demand, excess-supply respectively, of the bank's customers measured in EUR millions, too. Number of trades is decomposed into an expected and an unexpected component by a standard ARMA (1,1) process in accordance to Galati (2003). Realized exchange rate volatility is calculated by summing up squared exchange rate returns every minute for a whole day using the Olsen data set. Quoted spreads are the span between the best bid and ask quote every minute, averaged out on a daily basis. Estimation uses ordinary least squares with a Newey-West HAC standard errors and covariance controlling for heteroscedasticity. T-values are reported in the 3rd column, and "***", "**" and "*" indicate significance at the 1%, 5% and 10%-level respectively.

Now we turn our attention to the events of September 11th. In Table 4.4 we test if the above relationships are disturbed at that time. We assume that effects of September 11th lasted no longer than until September 17th as the financial business went back to normal on Monday 17th, when all the US financial markets reopened. Therefore we create a dummy-variable which takes a value equal to one on September 11th to September 14th and zero otherwise. Table 4.4A not only shows that the positive correlation between trading activity and volatility holds, but also that it actually intensifies. The strong significant positive coefficient of number of trades is almost doubled, adjusted R^2 increases by more than 200 percent. This contrasts with the mixed results of Galati (2003, Table 8, page 21). In his study this relationship breaks down in times of stress for some emerging market countries, indicating a lack of liquidity. Apparently, this is not the case here. In Panel B we have divided daily number of trades into interbank and customer trades as customer and interbank trading activities might be of different importance. Whereas interbank trading shows the familiar relationship between volume and volatility, which intensifies during the September 11th events, customer trading explicitly seems to calm the market during this period of stress. Customer trading activity at our bank contributes to a decrease in exchange rate volatility during the events on a statistically significant level, whereas at other times it has no significant influence at all.

In Panels C, D and E we look at the bid-ask spreads. There is no disruption of the general relationship either. Volatility and number of trades are positively correlated with the spread-size (see Panel C). Similarly to the more general results of Table 4.3, a split-up of number of trades into an expected and an unexpected component does not provide new insights as both are significantly positively correlated with quoted spreads (see Panel D). Unfortunately, a further partition of the variable "number of trades" into interbank and customer trades while accounting for the September 11th events at the same time sets boundaries to our estimation due to the limited observation base of only 87 trading days (see Panel E). Although the coefficients are signed accordingly to the results of Table 4.3B and C, they turn out to be statistically insignificant.

Table 4.4　Test for structural changes in daily data for USD/EUR

A　Realized volatility and number of trades

Dependent Variable: Realized exchange rate volatility		
Variable	Coefficient	t-Statistic
Constant	-0.324	-1.53
Log of number of trades, September 11th – September 14th	***0.315	3.18
Log of number of trades	***0.172	2.89
AR(1)	*0.164	1.76
Adjusted R^2	0.40	
Observations	86	

B　Realized volatility, interbank and customer trades

Dependent Variable: Realized exchange rate volatility		
Variable	Coefficient	t-Statistic
Constant	-0.108	-1.26
Log of number of interbank trades, September 11th – September 14th	***1.164	7.91
Log of number of interbank trades	***0.121	3.61
Log of number of customer trades, September 11th – September 14th	***-1.545	-6.62
Log of number of customer trades	-0.001	-0.03
AR(1)	-0.056	-0.33
Adjusted R^2	0.67	
Observations	86	

The dependent variable is the realized exchange rate volatility each day. Number of trades is the overall number of foreign exchange deal transacted at the small German bank each day. Estimation uses a dummy-variable, which takes the value one for September 11th to 14th, zero otherwise. Number of trades is divided into customer and interbank trades in Panel B. Realized exchange rate volatility is calculated by summing up squared exchange rate returns every minute for a whole day using the Olsen data set. Estimation uses ordinary least squares with a Newey-West HAC standard errors and covariance controlling for heteroscedasticity. T-values are reported in the 3rd column, and "***", "**" and "*" indicate significance at the 1%, 5% and 10%-level respectively. We obtain similar results for GBP/EUR and CHF/EUR when using number of ticks instead of number of trades.

Table 4.4 Test for structural changes in daily data for USD/EUR (continued)

C Spread, realized volatility and number of trades

Dependent Variable: Quoted spread

Variable	Coefficient	t-Statistic
Constant	***1.154	4.78
Realized exchange rate volatility, September 11th – September 14th	***1.216	5.92
Realized exchange rate volatility	***1.998	6.25
Log of number of trades, September 11th – September 14th	***0.352	4.13
Log of number of trades	**0.166	2.11
Adjusted R^2	0.67	
Observations	87	

D Spread, realized volatility, expected and unexpected number of trades

Dependent Variable: Quoted spread

Variable	Coefficient	t-Statistic
Constant	0.495	1.11
Realized exchange rate volatility, September 11th – September 14th	***2.369	28.10
Realized exchange rate volatility	***1.951	6.33
Log of expected number of trades, September 11th – September 14th	**0.311	2.51
Log of expected number of trades	**0.350	2.63
Log of unexpected number of trades, September 11th – September 14th	**0.250	2.06
Log of unexpected number of trades	***0.345	2.65
Adjusted R^2	0.74	
Observations	86	

E Spreads, realized volatility, interbank and customer trades

Dependent Variable: Quoted spread

Variable	Coefficient	t-Statistic
Constant	***1.324	6.24
Realized exchange rate volatility, September 11th – September 14th	0.733	1.02
Realized exchange rate volatility	***2.038	6.60
Log of number of interbank trades, September 11th – September 14th	0.971	1.23
Log of number of interbank trades	0.069	0.79
Log of number of customer trades, September 11th – September 14th	-0.916	-0.89
Log of number of customer trades	0.091	1.38
Adjusted R^2	0.67	
Observations	87	

As a final test of whether there was a substantial change in the above relation-ships, we carry out a Chow (1960) Breakpoint Test on the volume-volatility re-lation. The Chow Test is commonly used to test for structural breaks in the pa-rameters of a model in cases where the disturbance term is assumed to be the same in both periods. Table 4.5 shows that we cannot reject the null hypothesis that the first 44 observations have the same linear structure as the last 42 obser-vations. Thus, September 11th did not have a permanent effect on the determi-nants of foreign exchange trading. There is no structural break in the data. The market proved to be very liquid given the assumed relations.

Table 4.5   Chow Breakpoint Tests for the volatility-volume relation

Dependent Variable: Realized exchange rate volatility		
Variable	Coefficient	t-Statistic
Constant	-0.301	-1.54
Log of number of trades	***0.172	2.85
Adjusted R^2	0.11	
Observations	87	

Chow Breakpoint Test: September 11th			
F-statistic	1.94	Probability	0.15

Chow (1960) Breakpoint Test tests for structural breaks in the parameters of the regression of number of trades on realized volatility. It is assumed that the disturbance term is the same in both periods. The F-statistic shows that we cannot reject the null hypothesis that the first 44 observations have the same linear structure as the last 42 observations.

How long did the foreign exchange markets deal with the issue? To check the persistence of the events we carry out VAR analyses for the volatility and the bid-ask spread in the USD/EUR, GBP/EUR and CHF/EUR market (Figure 4.3). Effects of September 11th on the volatility and spreads vanish after a few days only. The impact on the exchange rate volatilities differs between curren-cies. Not surprisingly, the USD/EUR volatility reacts most strongly, whereas the CHF/EUR volatility's reaction is only half the size. The impact becomes statisti-cally insignificant after roughly one day for all currencies.[50] The impact on spreads is roughly the same for all three currency pairs. Probably due to the proximity of markets to the events the effect on the CHF/EUR spread already disappears after one day whereas the USD/EUR spread is back to its normal

---

50   We used the lagged volatility and spreads in order to be able to carry out an analysis of current variables as VAR analyses use only lagged terms.

level not until approximately three days after. Ordinary least squares regressions using day-dummies confirm these results (not reported here). Summing up, the foreign USD/EUR exchange market functioned well. It easily digested the increased exchange rate risk after this incomprehensible tragedy.

Figure 4.3 Persistence of September 11th – Effect by means of VAR impulse responses

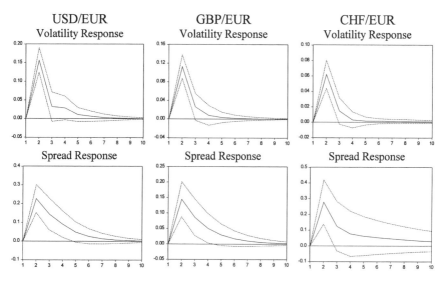

Plot shows simultaneous VAR impulse responses of realized volatility and spread for USD/EUR, GBP/EUR and CHF/EUR to September 11th, i.e. a dummy-variable which takes the value one on September 11th, zero otherwise, on a daily basis. Dashed lines represent the plus/minus two standard deviation bands, alongside the impulse responses.

4.3.3 Having a closer look at the high-frequency data

Apparently, the shock of the September 11th events must have been absorbed within a very short time span – maybe within hours or even minutes. To study these very short-term relationships we generate another data set on a ten-minute basis. From September 10th to September 12th we add up all observations for the relevant variables every ten minutes from 8:00 to 18:00 (MET).[51]

---

51 After September 12th there has been a change in collecting the data at Olsen Financial Technologies. Therefore we cannot include more days after September 11th for these kinds of analyses. To produce symmetry we limit the data to one day before and one day after September 11th.

Figure 4.4 gives a first impression of what actually happened on the USD/EUR foreign exchange market on September 11th. The first news about a plane-crash into the World Trade Center was received in Central Europe at 14:40 (MET). Our bank usually ended its business day before 18:00 (MET). We have highlighted this period in the graphs, i.e. 14:40 to 18:00 (MET) on September 11th. Panel A shows that there was a sharp depreciation of the USD during the events, though the exchange rate returned back to its normal level during the morning of the following day. In Panels C and E we can see that the realized exchange rate volatility as well as the number of trades increased erratically in the afternoon of September 11th. Both curves calm down the very next day. According to the number of trades, the number of ticks increases rapidly, too (see Panel B). Underneath, you can see that the quoted spread size roughly triples due to the events of September 11th. The downward sloping of this curve takes more time than for the realized volatility – a result consistent with the VAR analyses of Figure 4.3. Absolute customer order imbalances had been remarkably high during the afternoon of September 11th. Two additional comments are noteworthy here. First, from September 11th to September 14th there was no financial customer business at our small bank at all.[52] All trades during that period were conducted by commercial customers. Second, the observed order imbalances stem from extensive USD purchases – going along with a depreciation of the USD. This is consistent with Mende, Menkhoff and Osler (2004). They show that commercial customer order flow has a negative effect on the price movement as these customers can be considered as uninformed. It is also consistent with Bjønnes, Rime and Solheim (2003), who show that non-bank customers often take the other market side and hence provide liquidity. In Panels I and J of Figure 4.4 we have contrasted number of trades with number of ticks and realized exchange rate volatility. Above (Panels G and H), we have connected customer order imbalances to the exchange rate and volatility. One can spot bank and customer variables exhibiting a lagged reaction structure to the events – somehow "following" the general market movements – although we cannot fully confirm this notion statistically.[53] Therefore, we cannot conclude that causality runs strictly from the market to the bank.

---

52 This may be due to the close-down of many US financial markets until Monday September-ber 17th as financial customers trade way more in foreign stocks than commercial customers. It may also be an indication of different risk perceptions of financial and commercial customers.

53 We perform Granger Causality Tests, which unfortunately do not reveal clear-cut results in this manner (see Annex 4.2).

Figure 4.4 Foreign USD/EUR exchange trading determinants during September 10th – 12th

A Exchange rate

B Number of ticks

C Realized exchange rate volatility

D Bid-ask spread

E Number of trades

F Customer order imbalances

G Exchange rate and customer order imbalances

H Volatility and customer order imbalances

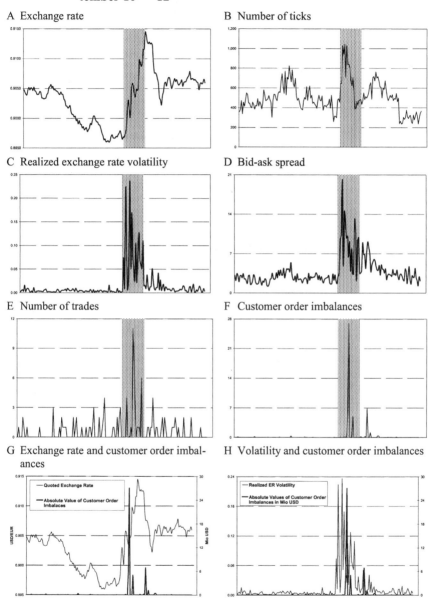

I   Number of ticks and number of trades   J   Volatility and number of trades

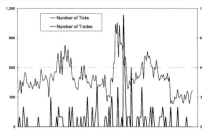
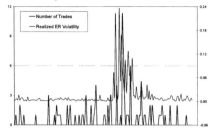

Figure shows USD/EUR trading determinants taken from the Olsen data set and from the small bank's trading record from September 10th to September 12th 2001 on a basis of ten minutes intervals. September 11th 14:40 – 18:00 (MET) is marked grey.

To test whether the volume-volatility-spread relation breaks down intra-day, we carry out regressions similar to the ones in Table 4.4. Table 4.6 reports the results. To measure trading activity we now refer to number of ticks instead of number of trades. On a ten-minute interval basis there are just not enough observations to produce significant results.[54] The results in Table 4.6 show that the positive correlations between volume and volatility on the one hand, and volume, volatility and spreads on the other hand do in fact boost during the events of September 11th. The increasing influence of trading activity on volatility and unexpected number of ticks on spreads especially indicate the massive arrival of new information and the enormous raise in price risk due to general uncertainty. No doubt it was a turbulent afternoon on the USD/EUR foreign exchange market. The uncertainty, however, did not last very long and the market pretty much returned to everyday life after only half a day.

---

54   Besides, the cointegration relation between ticks and trades disappears on an intra-day basis (not reported here). There is rather a lagged connection between the market as a whole and the trading activity of a single bank than simultaneous co-movement (see Annex 4.2).

Table 4.6 Structural Changes in 10 minutes interval data for USD/EUR

A   Realized exchange rate volatility and number of ticks

Dependent Variable: Realized exchange rate volatility		
Variable	Coefficient	t-Statistic
Constant	*-0.043	-1.73
Log of number of ticks	**0.008	1.98
Log of number of ticks during the events of September 11th	***0.019	4.29
AR(1)	***-0.233	-3.05
Adjusted R^2	0.55	
Observations	179	

B   Spread, realized exchange rate volatility and number of ticks

Dependent Variable: Quoted spread		
Variable	Coefficient	t-Statistic
Constant	***-9.155	-3.11
Realized exchange rate volatility	***144.603	8.22
Realized exchange rate volatility during the events of September 11th	***29.181	3.27
Log of number of ticks	***1.855	3.86
Log of number of ticks during the events of September 11th	***2.369	4.07
AR(1)	-0.155	-1.64
Adjusted R^2	0.65	
Observations	179	

C   Spread, realized exchange rate volatility, expected and unexpected number of ticks

Dependent Variable: Quoted spread		
Variable	Coefficient	t-Statistic
Constant	***-10.095	-2.87
Realized exchange rate volatility	***133.500	7.00
Realized exchange rate volatility during the events of September 11th	***25.597	3.18
Log of number of expected ticks	***2.020	3.51
Log of number of expected ticks during the events of September 11th	***2.524	3.99
Log of number of unexpected ticks	***0.786	2.67
Log of number of unexpected ticks during the events of September 11th	**7.785	2.33
AR(1)	-0.001	-0.01
Adjusted R^2	0.67	
Observations	178	

Variables are summed up, averaged out respectively, every ten minutes. Estimation uses a dummy-variable, which takes the value one for September 11th between 14:40 and 18:00 (MET), zero otherwise. The dependent variable is realized volatility, quoted spread respectively. Number of ticks is the overall number of quotes. Number of ticks is decomposed into an expected and an unexpected component by a standard ARMA (1,1) process in accordance to Galati (2003). Estimation uses ordinary least squares with a Newey-West HAC standard errors and covariance controlling for heteroscedasticity. T-values are reported in the 3rd column, and "***", "**" and "*" indicate significance at the 1%, 5% and 10%-level respectively.

4.4 Conclusion

This study of the relationship between foreign exchange trading activities, exchange rate volatility and bid-ask spreads on the foreign exchange market during the events of September 11th was conducted on the basis of a unique data set, consisting of actual trading data of a small bank in Germany and market-wide quoted data. To our knowledge there is no other study existent which examines these relationships around September 11th. We find that the general connection between trading volume and volatility does not break down due to the attacks. Whether we look at the daily data or at the intra-day data does not make a difference. The positive correlation between number of trades, number of ticks respectively, and realized volatility becomes even stronger during the time of stress. The same holds for the relation between volume, volatility and spreads. Although some variables, such as the volatility and spreads, multiply in the course of the events, there is no structural break in the data. The shock merely persists for up to three days.

We also look at the bank's intra-day variables trying to learn about the trading behavior of market participants. There is some evidence that our bank reacts to the increased market-wide quoting activity and that commercial customers were in the end taking the other market side and hence providing liquidity. This would be in line with findings of Bjønnes, Rime and Solheim (2003), Fan and Lyons (2003), and Mende, Menkhoff and Osler (2004).

We conclude that foreign exchange markets for key currencies, such as USD/EUR, GBP/EUR and CHF/EUR, can be considered as very liquid ones – unlike emerging markets' foreign exchange markets (see Galati, 2003). This is simply due to the huge number of market participants and due to the sheer size of their daily turnovers. Especially the decentralized build-up of these markets assures sufficient liquidity and market efficiency.

Annex 4.1   Realized exchange rate volatility, trading activity and weekday dummies

Dependent Variable: Realized exchange rate volatility

Variable	Coefficient	t-Statistic
Constant	-0.419	-1.32
Log of number of trades	**0.195	2.12
Tuesday	0.062	0.77
Wednesday	0.044	1.13
Thursday	0.025	0.76
Friday	0.043	1.20
AR(1)	***0.270	4.56
Adjusted R^2	0.13	
Observations	86	

Annex 4.2   Granger causality tests on trade and quote data variables on a 10 minutes interval basis

	F-statistic	Probability	
Realized volatility does not cause USD/EUR	2.63	0.03	**
USD/EUR does not cause realized volatility	1.30	0.27	
Customer order imbalance does not cause USD/EUR	8.75	0.00	***
USD/EUR does not cause customer order imbalance	1.99	0.08	*
Number of ticks does not cause USD/EUR	0.99	0.43	
USD/EUR does not cause number of ticks	0.47	0.80	
Number of trades does not cause USD/EUR	4.18	0.00	***
USD/EUR does not cause number of trades	5.23	0.00	***
Spread does not cause USD/EUR	0.76	0.58	
USD/EUR does not cause spread	2.54	0.03	**
Customer order imbalance does not cause realized volatility	3.21	0.01	***
Realized volatility does not cause customer order imbalance	17.49	0.00	***
Number of ticks does not cause realized volatility	6.14	0.00	***
Realized volatility does not cause number of ticks	2.24	0.05	*
Number of trades does not cause realized volatility	6.85	0.00	***
Realized volatility does not cause number of trades	12.33	0.00	***
Spread does not cause realized volatility	5.92	0.00	***
Realized volatility does not cause spread	10.51	0.00	***
Number of ticks does not cause customer order imbalance	1.99	0.08	*
Customer order imbalance does not cause number of ticks	0.96	0.44	
Number of trades does not cause customer order imbalance	31.94	0.00	***
Customer order imbalance does not cause number of trades	0.88	0.50	
Spread does not cause customer order imbalance	4.81	0.00	***
Customer order imbalance does not cause spread	6.72	0.00	***
Number of trades does not cause number of ticks	1.48	0.20	
Number of ticks does not cause number of trades	2.85	0.02	**
Spread does not cause number of ticks	0.91	0.48	
Number of ticks does not cause spread	3.34	0.01	***
Spread does not cause number of trades	4.87	0.00	***
Number of trades does not cause spread	1.93	0.09	*

5   Tobin Tax Effects Seen from the Foreign Exchange Market's Microstructure*

5.1   Introduction

The Tobin tax ranks high on the agenda for many non-governmental organizations (NGOs), trade unions, political parties and even governments, but has remained comparatively under-researched by academia. A major exception in this respect is the volume edited by ul Haq, Kaul and Grunberg (1996), reflecting the debate surrounding an expert meeting in 1995.[55] This volume covers a wide range of issues and conflicting views. Among them is Jeffrey Frankel's (1996) paper addressing the core question whether a Tobin tax might help to heal market shortcomings. The novelty of his contribution is to introduce the concept of market microstructure to the Tobin tax discussion. As the microstructure concept has led to a wealth of fruitful research over the last few years (see e.g. Lyons, 2001a; Sarno and Taylor, 2001), it provides a motivation for continuing Frankel's approach by drawing on the most recent results (see also Lyons, 2001b). It can be shown that the traditional Tobin tax concept is not viable in the light of new findings.

The motivations for endorsing a Tobin tax proposal vary widely and may serve various concerns. Some proponents would like to curb the welfare-reducing waste of resources for speculative activities (Arestis and Sawyer, 1997), while others see the Tobin tax as a means to putting pressure on banks' profits (Wahl and Waldow, 2001). It is likely that many of today's proponents – including several governments and parliaments – have in mind the income generating potential of this tax, which they believe should be directed towards the needs of the poor (see ul Haq et al., 1996; Reisen, 2002). This paper does not discuss these and other motivations, but concentrates on financial market aspects. Tobin's idea was to guide decision-making in foreign exchange in such a way that the overwhelming amount of short-term transactions would be restricted in favor of longer-term oriented transactions. Although this guidance objective could be adequately addressed by a proportional tax on all foreign exchange transactions, the academic discussion has revealed a non-trivial price:

*   I would like to thank my co-author Lukas Menkhoff (University of Hannover, Germany). This paper was originally published under the title "Tobin tax effects seen from the foreign exchange market's microstructure" in *International Finance* 6, 2003, pp.227-247, and is reproduced by kind permission of Blackwell Publishing Ltd. Oxford. We would also like to thank Michael Frömmel, Jochen Michaelis, seminar participants in Stuttgart-Hohenheim, and two anonymous referees for their helpful comments, in particular one very constructive contribution.

55   This effort was organized by individuals linked to the UNDP, with Barry Eichengreen as lead consultant.

the reduction in short-term transactions can markedly reduce market liquidity, which will in turn most probably increase volatility. Increased volatility means that gains from foreign trade cannot be realized because of the higher exchange rate risk and the widening spreads. The consequent conflict between the objectives of "guidance" and "liquidity" must therefore be addressed. Market microstructure research provides some useful insights in this respect.

As Frankel and Rose (1995) and Taylor (1995) have noted, the failure of traditional exchange rate modeling to explain shorter-term price movements provides a powerful motivation to search for new avenues, such as microstructure research. Two strands of this research program are clearly related to the issues raised by a Tobin tax. First, studies have differentiated the frequently assumed assumption of a representative agent forming perfectly rational expectations, and have instead suggested heterogeneous agents with different behavior (see e.g. Sarno and Taylor, 2001). Second, studies have examined the impact of certain actions on the market and postulate the existence of "high impact" market participants (Fan and Lyons, 2003). The objective of this paper is to make fruitful use of this literature to clarify the relation between the above-mentioned conflicting objectives of guidance and liquidity.

We find that the conception of foreign exchange markets that implicitly underlies the Tobin tax proposal is misleading under the current circumstances. At least three groups need to be differentiated, i.e. banks, asset managers, and commercial firms. Recent empirical evidence suggests that each of these groups behaves differently and has its own characteristic impact on the market. The role of banks in particular is at the same time overstated and underrated: banks do not speculate as assumed, but their dealing desks are essential in providing liquidity and allocating risks. We argue that it is rather the asset managers who have most probably become the main force moving shorter-term exchange rates.[56] They are the true kingpins of foreign exchange markets, and should be the focus of any appropriate Tobin taxing. Finally, commercial customers would appear to be less relevant for the shorter-term issues being addressed here.[57]

Beyond these new insights into the behavior of participating groups, coupled with changes in the composition of the participants, another relevant innovation in the foreign exchange market is the further decline in transaction costs. We use exemplary data to illustrate the minimal spreads that have now been reached. Recent market microstructure research has uncovered these changes, which completely alter the implication to be drawn for the functionality of any Tobin tax.

---

56 Following the BIS studies about market shares in foreign exchange, asset managers have gained importance at the cost of banks (see also section 3.1).

57 Nevertheless, commercial customers are playing an important liquidity role at the daily frequency and lower, as indicated for example by Bjønnes, Rime and Solheim (2003).

We conclude – in contrast to Frankel (1996) and Eichengreen (1996, pp.278 et sqq.)[58] – that a proportional Tobin tax applied to all transactions cannot help solve the conflicting goals: a low tax rate does not influence decision making by asset managers, whereas any noticeable tax burden will damage liquidity provisioning. There is no tax rate that would be able to simultaneously satisfy both the guidance and the liquidity objectives. Consequently, the Tobin tax issue remains live up to this day but the concept of a Tobin tax in its present form is not advisable on economic grounds. The question of whether it can be usefully reformulated is a matter for further research.

We proceed in three steps. Section 5.2 outlines the original Tobin tax concept in order to gain hypotheses that can be empirically tested. Theoretically justified hypotheses are confronted with empirical findings of microstructure research in Section 5.3. Section 5.4 concludes with policy considerations.

5.2   The Tobin tax concept

James Tobin (1978) made his by now very prominent tax proposal as president of the Eastern Economic Association in 1978, when he detailed the general idea that he had already advanced in 1972. Its roots go even deeper into the history of economic reasoning, most prominently the statement by Keynes (1936) that transaction taxes on financial assets might help dampen economically unjustified speculation and thus reduce volatility. Although this objective of volatility reduction is at the forefront of economic discussion nowadays, it was not Tobin's major motivation when floating his proposal. Instead, his main focus was on increasing the space for national economic policy making, in particular for monetary policy. The tax was primarily seen as a means to sever the links between national currencies.

As an important side-aspect, however, Tobin discussed the shortcomings of flexible exchange rates as they really are. Most important from his viewpoint is a distinction into "mechanically efficient" markets which lack anchoring in fundamentals (elaborated further in Tobin, 1984). According to his analysis, it is short-term oriented, self-referential speculation by banks that drives exchange rates away from fundamentals.

The background to this view from the 1970s is the emergence of the international financial markets that were fostered by the floating of major exchange rates between 1971 and 1973. It became obvious that foreign exchange markets are not really mirrors of international flows of goods and foreign direct investments. Rather, it is financial flows that determine exchange rates over relevant horizons, as the famous Dornbusch model has explicitly demonstrated (see

---

58   "... a transaction cost of 1% ... can have major effects on the location, nature and volume of trading. Fortunately, as we have demonstrated, the effect of a 0.1% tax in investments with moderately long-term horizons would be small, while the effect on very short-term transactions would be large." (Frankel, 1996, p.65)

117

Rogoff, 2002, for an acknowledgment). Financial flows adjust to expectations, which make their reaction to changes in environment quicker than for goods flows, and also make them sensitive to rumors and other non-fundamental influences. Tobin's skepticism against the fundamental evaluation efficiency of foreign exchange markets corresponds well to the failure of relevant modeling efforts. Although advances have been made, and although exchange rates do react to news and regime changes, the task of formulating an exchange rate model based on macro fundamentals that holds – or even holds out-of-sample – has yet not been mastered (see e.g. Neely and Sarno, 2002).

The advent of microstructure research in the 1990s has, however, led to serious doubts about this notion of destabilizing bank speculation. In particular, Frankel (1996) has made the point that the high trading volume of banks is due to their intermediation function in decentralized markets. Their dealing desks trade foreign exchange in order to allocate open positions to those market participants who are willing to hold them. As part of this process, large orders are chunked into smaller lots that will more readily be accepted by risk-averse agents. This function of banks in foreign exchange markets is crucial from an economic perspective, as it ensures liquidity that serves to allocate risks and dampen volatility.

Besides a dealing desk, many banks also operate a proprietary trading desk.[59] The behavior of the two desks differs, as the purpose of the latter is to generate profits from position holding and, possibly, arbitrage activities. The horizon is thus typically longer than that of the "regular" dealing desk, and its overall behavior is closer to that of asset managers. Seen from our analytical point of view, proprietary trading can be thus regarded as a specific subset of asset managers, and less so as a variation of the banks' other dealing activities.

The most important consequence of the debate relating to the provision of liquidity by bank dealing desks was a further decline in the proposed tax rate. Whereas Tobin (1978) originally mentioned a rate of 1%, and subsequently published a rate of 0.5% (Eichengreen, Tobin and Wyplosz, 1995), initial microstructure findings suggest even lower rates. In the volume by ul Haq et al. (1996), the discussion centers around a range of 0.05% to 0.25%, with 0.1% as the figure mentioned most frequently (see Eichengreen, 1996). The purpose of this low tax rate is twofold: first, it is intended to limit incentives for tax avoidance; and second, a low rate should ensure the smooth functioning of the interbank market even after introduction of the tax.

We take this state of the debate as our reference point to derive four hypotheses about the perceived functioning of the foreign exchange market and the expected effect of introducing the Tobin tax. These hypotheses are formulated in

---

59 One referee rightly suggested making this differentiation in the trading activities of banks.

a way to make them testable by new evidence from microstructure research.[60] The starting point is the idea that foreign exchange markets are often considered to consist of two major groups: "good" firms engaged in foreign trade, and "bad" banks speculating on short-term horizons.

H1   Banks dominate the foreign exchange market by volume. They act on very short-term horizons and speculate heavily.

A second important concern for justifying a Tobin tax is the argument that the short-term horizons do not reflect the most efficient ways of collecting and using fundamental news. Rather, there is a suggestion that short-term horizons are related to the use of non-fundamental information. This kind of information is extraneous to exchange rate determination as specified in macro models, such as technical analysis.

H2   Short-term horizons indicate the use of non-fundamental information.

Finally, the introduction of a proportional Tobin tax has its strongest effect on shorter-term oriented trading activities, and thus generates an incentive towards longer-term views in position taking. As longer-term speculation is regarded as a distinctly more stabilizing activity – in the sense of reaching fundamentally justified exchange rates – than shorter-term speculation, which causes rather erratic or self-enforcing deviations from fundamentals, a Tobin tax corrects a distorted decision-making calculus. The effects of this "correction" would be more fundamentally based exchange rates, fewer or less severe bubbles, and thus a lower level of (excessive) volatility.

H3   A Tobin tax reduces excessive exchange rate volatility.

So far, these three hypotheses refer to the guidance of foreign exchange markets. A Tobin tax is seen as an appropriate measure to ensure more fundamentally based exchange rates. Even if one accepts this position, there is the problem of the liquidity objective. The discussion referred to above has led to the conclusion that a tax rate of 0.1% would be able to provide a solution to the conflicting goals: with this rate, it is claimed, decisions will be oriented more significantly towards fundamentals without distorting the existing market structure. In short, there is a tax rate that simultaneously satisfies both the guidance and the liquidity objectives.

---

60   Our intention with these hypotheses is to cover the core aspects comprehensively. Further advances in microstructure research might provide even better tests of these four hypotheses.

H4 A tax rate of about 0.1% satisfies both the guidance and the liquidity objectives.

In summary, the first three hypotheses reflect the state of thinking by Tobin tax proponents, such as Eichengreen, Tobin and Wyplosz (1995), before the UNDP expert meeting in 1995, whereas the fourth hypothesis takes the findings of Frankel (1996) and related work into account (see Eichengreen, 1996). In the following sections, we test these hypotheses by drawing on available material.

5.3 Confronting the Tobin tax hypotheses with recent market microstructure findings

This section uses two sources of material for hypothesis tests. First, available findings from the literature are applied to the Tobin tax issues, following the lead taken by Frankel, who has bridged these two strands of literature. Second, we use certain additional material from our own empirical studies to complement other data. The structure of the analysis matches the four hypotheses introduced in Section 5.2.

5.3.1 Do banks dominate the market through short-term speculation?

The notion of speculating banks that dominate foreign exchange markets has its basis in the ratio between foreign exchange transactions and international goods trade. This ratio has mushroomed since the late 1970s, and is now in the region of about 50. It seems an obvious conclusion that those transactions which do not serve the goods trade must largely be of a speculative nature. The suspects for this speculation are banks that intermediate their customers' needs. To clarify the issues involved, hypothesis 1 is split into its three logical components, i.e. banks dominate, they act at short-term notice, and they mainly speculate.

In terms of the dominance of the banks, the Bank for International Settlements produces a survey study every three years which provides information about the market share of the main groups in the foreign exchange market, among other things. According to this source (BIS, 2002), the share taken by banks ("reporting dealers" in the BIS terminology) is still the largest, at 59%. However, the relative importance of these market makers is declining, and the shooting stars are "other financial institutions", which rank now second (28%), outpacing "non financial customers", with a 13% share.[61] It is thus obvious, that banks still dominate volumes – not by a ratio of 98% to 2%, but rather by about 60% to 40% – and that their share is in decline.

---

61 "Other financial institutions" are those who are not "reporting dealers", including non-market making banks, pension funds etc.

The second component of hypothesis 1, i.e. short-term orientation, can be also verified and does not require any qualification. The few available studies since the 1990s that precisely document the behavior of single FX dealers all reveal very short-term behavior. To show this in a graphical form, we have plotted the net positions, i.e. the inventory, of two dealers in Figure 5.1. The left-hand graph presents the large US dealers initially surveyed, with figures from August 1992 (Lyons, 1995). The right-hand graph shows a medium-sized dealer from Germany with data from September 2001 (Mende and Menkhoff, 2003b). Although nine years have now passed, and despite their different size and business structure, it is directly obvious that both dealers – who should be regarded as liquidity dealers rather than proprietary traders – follow short-term strategies and change their position frequently. Even the sign of their net positions switches several times per day. This short-term orientation is unanimously confirmed by all available studies and can be thus regarded as a stylized fact of FX trading behavior by banks (see also Yao, 1998a; and Bjønnes and Rime, 2001b).

Figure 5.1   Foreign exchange inventories of a market maker and a small dealer

Market maker

Small dealer

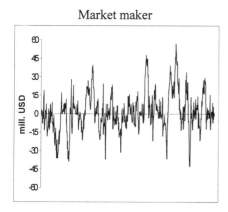
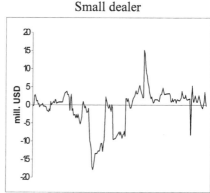

Plot of a market maker's inventory in millions of USD at the time of each incoming order during the sample week, 08/03/92 – 08/07/92.

Source: Lyons (1995)

Plot of a small dealer's inventory in millions of USD at the time of each order during the sample week, 09/03/01 – 09/07/01.

Source: Mende and Menkhoff (2003b)

121

This leads to the third component of hypothesis 1: that the foreign exchange business of banks mainly entails speculation. A look at Figure 5.1 gives rise to doubts about this proposition, and skepticism is nurtured by further facts. The above-mentioned studies indicate that dealers usually close or drastically reduce their open positions at the close of day. Figures from the one FX dealer study covering the longest period, i.e. four months of trading, reveal a clear picture (data from Mende and Menkhoff, 2003b):[62] on a daily volume of roughly 50 million USD/EUR trading, this bank has a median open position of only about 2 million USD, and the median of the daily closing position is a meager 1 million USD.

Figure 5.1 demonstrates not only comparatively low open positions, but also frequent marked reversals. Calculating the half-life of open positions further questions the notion of speculative behavior. All available studies again show unanimously that this half-life is measured only in minutes, implying that banks attempt to reduce open positions not just during the day, but also within intervals of minutes (see Figure 5.2). Thus, it should be obvious that position taking by banks cannot move foreign exchange markets beyond the extremely short-term intra-day horizon (see also Lyons, 2001a, p.246).[63] Nevertheless, the trades by dealers are signals through which the market learns about the underlying positions taken by participants with longer horizons (Evans and Lyons, 2002). When it comes to short-term daily movements, banks themselves do not take appreciable open positions at this horizon. Is there another group that could be responsible for changing open positions and that might influence exchange rate movements?

Microstructure research has indeed an answer to this important question. In a first approach, Evans and Lyons (2002) use data from daily aggregated order flows. For a four-month period, they have shown that cumulating the order flow in the DEM/USD (and the YEN/USD) market over time produces a net demand curve that is clearly related to the exchange rate.[64] This indicates that net buying orders for a currency drive its value upwards. This finding has been confirmed by following the cumulative customer orders of a large US market maker over nearly six years (Lyons, 2001a, p.249 et sqq.). Mende and Menkhoff (2003b) confirm the central role of customer order flow in the USD/EUR market for more disaggregated deal-by-deal data over a period of four months. Order

---

62 This kind of study covers comparatively short time-periods, as they are very rich in information regarding single trades. Most microstructure studies use less disaggregated or less complete data.

63 Only proprietary traders may exert some influence on longer horizons, in the same way as other asset managers.

64 The order flow is defined as the "net of buyer-initiated and seller-initiated orders; it is a measure of net buying pressure" (Evans and Lyons, 2002, p.171). In that study, only the direction of orders is measured, while the amount is not taken into account.

flows are thus a powerful source of information when it comes to explaining short-term exchange rate changes (see also Evans, 2002).

Figure 5.2   Reduction of open positions and implied half-lives

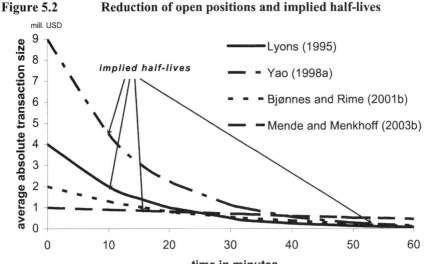

Note: This figure shows the behavior of four dealers from four different studies in a highly stylized way. The starting points are transactions of average size and the curved lines indicate the typical reduction of open positions over time. The half-lives of open positions resulting from typical behavior are marked.

The latest research indicates even more interesting information, as the order flow is split into several groups in the market. For a case study environment, Lyons (2001a, p.256 et sqq.) finds that "financial institutions" (in particular fund managers) are the group whose changes in net position are closely related to the YEN/USD rate at shorter-term horizons (the same data are analyzed in more detail in Fan and Lyons, 2003). The financial institutions mentioned here are the same as the "other financial institutions" in the BIS (2002) study, which the BIS defines in particular as asset managers. We will stick to this latter intuitively understandable term of asset managers.

The state of knowledge regarding hypothesis 1 can thus be summarized as one of partial rejection. Banks still dominate FX trading volume and they behave in a very short-term manner. However, the central component of hypothesis 1, that banks speculate and thus move exchange rates, must be rejected by the available evidence. It is not the banks (nor is it commercial customers) which "make" the market, and there are pointers that indicate that asset managers play the central role. It is thus most interesting to learn about the foundations of their decision-making.

5.3.2 Do short-term horizons indicate non-fundamentalism?

The relevance of short-term horizons to decision-making and the use of non-fundamental information have a certain intuitive appeal, but is not compelling. It could well be that short-term trading reflects changing evaluations which cover infinite horizons. The survey of London chief dealers by Taylor and Allen (1992) provided systematic evidence for the first time. It found that technical analysis dominates forecasting horizons of up to a few days, whereas fundamental analysis only dominates decision-making for long-term horizons. Moreover, the majority of participants made it clear that they focus on the shorter term. This finding has been replicated several times in the literature and can thus be regarded as well confirmed (see Menkhoff, 1997, for Germany; Lui and Mole, 1998, for Hong Kong; Cheung and Chinn, 2001, for the US; and Cheung, Chinn and Marsh, 2000, for the UK).

Additional evidence supporting the notion of non-fundamental factors in the shorter-term has been provided by studies examining the term structure of exchange rate expectations (see more in Taylor, 1995). It can be regarded as a stylized fact that shorter-term exchange rate changes respond to lagged exchange rate changes in the same direction. By contrast, the same persons expect the opposite movement of exchange rates over longer-term horizons, such as three to 12 months. Froot and Ito (1989) find that this kind of expectation formation, the so called "expectation twist", does not actually fit their concept of "consistency", which may be seen as a weaker requirement than full-fledged rationality.

In a related attempt to measure relevant restrictions on the horizon of professionals, Menkhoff (2001) compares different horizons and finds results inconsistent with unrestricted behavior. In particular, the required time seen for fundamentals to succeed in the foreign exchange market is often longer than the horizons of the same persons when taking open positions. Thus, professionals do not fully use their available knowledge on fundamentals. Even more interestingly for our discussion, this restriction applies not only to dealers, but also to the international fund managers.

Finally, we show in Figure 5.3 the relative weight that dealers and fund managers assign to the use of fundamentals (in relation to technical analysis and flow analysis), depending on their typical decision-making horizon. The data come from a survey of German dealers and fund managers (Gehrig and Menkhoff, 2004). Again, those who are more short-term oriented do not regard fundamentals very highly, whereas the importance of fundamentals increases with the time horizon. Interestingly, this relation holds separately for dealers and fund managers. Fund managers have longer horizons and – related to this fact – rely more strongly on fundamentals. However, even fund managers cannot be regarded as trading purely on the basis of fundamentals, as this kind of information merely receives half of the weights allocated by the group members themselves.

In summary, there is more than adequate available evidence on the dominance of technical analysis over shorter horizons for FX dealers. Complementary evidence – in the form of extrapolative expectations and restricted horizons – also supports the notion of the limited influence of fundamentals on short-term horizons. The evidence on the significant group of international fund managers is thin, but in line with the findings for dealers, albeit to a somewhat lesser degree. Hypothesis 2 is thus supported by the evidence presented.

Figure 5.3   The importance of fundamentals at typical forecasting horizons

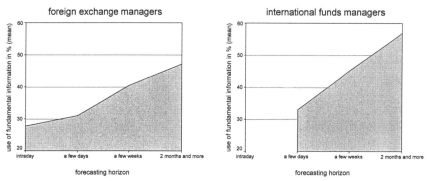

Note: The data stem from a questionnaire survey conducted in Germany in 2001 with about 200 responses. One question asks about the forecasting horizon when deciding on open foreign exchange positions. The other question asks about the relative weight assigned to fundamentals, technical analysis, and flows for typical decision-making in foreign exchange.

5.3.3   Does a Tobin tax reduce excessive exchange rate volatility?

The influence of heavy short-term non-fundamental trading on exchange rates cannot be expected to stabilize the market, although it may generate liquidity (see e.g. Kyle, 1985). The best that might happen is uncoordinated behavior by these individuals, with a result that many deals cancel each other out. It is, however, more probable that at least some of this trading involves participants who either react to the same signals or to each other. Survey evidence (Gehrig and Menkhoff, 2004), as well as a careful investigation of customer orders (Osler, 2003), supports this view. The consequence is that volatility increases compared with a market where trading is based only to fundamental news. Frankel (1996) has constructed a simple model from this idea.

He distinguishes two groups in the market: investors and speculators. The behavior of investors is oriented on the long term, and they trade only on deviations of the exchange rate from its fundamental equilibrium value. Speculators, by contrast, take a short-term view and buy a currency that is already (slightly) overvalued, i.e. they increase exchange rate bubbles. The total demand for the home currency is given by a function which captures the different behaviors of these two groups.

Now, assume that the actual exchange rate (expressed as units of home currency per one unit of foreign currency) is higher than its equilibrium value. Investors will then buy the home currency in order to depreciate the rate, whereas speculators will sell. The model does not give any answer regarding exchange rate dynamics, as the decisive parameters are exogenous. One could imagine that the weight of investors increases the more evident it is that the valuation is wrong, and that they behave more confidently under such circumstances. The model is designed to illustrate the benefit from a Tobin tax. The tax emerges as an instrument that strengthens demand by long-term investors following the introduction of the Tobin tax. Under these assumptions, a tax could indeed reduce exchange rate volatility.

Research in finance, however, has shown a counterbalancing effect. The introduction of a Tobin tax has the same impact as an increase in spreads. As order flow analyses have shown, this will hinder the trading process and the adjustment of prices to information (see Melvin and Yin, 2000).[65] Moreover, an increase in spreads obviously reduces liquidity, and less liquid markets tend to be more volatile, as idiosyncratic shocks generally tend to disturb orderly market conditions (e.g. Habermeier and Kirilenko, 2002; Hau, 2002). This point was also made in the UNDP volume (see ul Haq et al., 1996). Transaction costs have fallen further since then, and – even more importantly – the recent research on disentangled order flows of different groups of market participants has not been considered sufficiently in the Tobin tax discussion.

To demonstrate the possible effect of a Tobin tax, we have ordered all USD/EUR transactions of a smaller bank by the estimated spread, and calculated the same for interbank transactions only (direct and brokered trade; data from

---

65 As Melvin and Yin (2000) are able to identify a positive linkage between the arrival of public information and the FX market activity, they conclude that the trading process itself provides the function of adjusting prices and quantities in response to new public information.

Mende and Menkhoff, 2003b). Figure 5.4 shows that the spread is virtually always less than 100 pips, i.e. approximately 1%. It is more interesting that 99% of interbank dealing operates with a spread of less than 0.1%, and that 94% of interbank trading still takes place with a spread lower than 0.05%. This implies that even a Tobin tax as low as 0.1%, i.e. the preferred rate following the expert meeting in 1995, is greater than the highest realized spreads in the interbank market. When applying the elasticity calculations for stock markets suggested by Campbell and Froot (1994) to our case, the interbank market would shrink by more than 80% for a Tobin of 0.1% and an assumed elasticity of only -1.[66] Consequently, the present market structure could not easily continue to exist at this tax rate; liquidity would drop markedly and volatility would increase.

Which of the inconsistent effects might dominate is therefore unclear: would a Tobin tax strengthen fundamental speculation to such an extent that it overcompensates a rise in volatility caused by declining liquidity? There is no clear answer for hypothesis 3.

Figure 5.4   The cumulative distribution of spreads

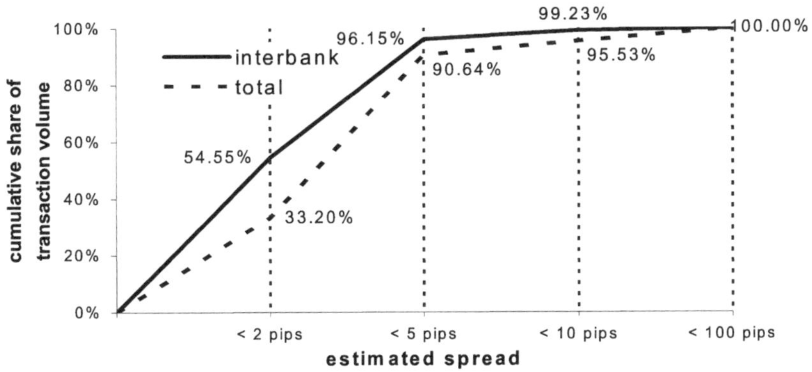

Note: The cumulative shares of transaction volume with an "estimated spread" of less than 2 pips, i.e. approximately 0.02%, less than 5 pips etc., are shown here for interbank trades and for total trades respectively. The "estimated spread" is calculated on the basis of the existing data set (Mende and Menkhoff, 2003b).

---

66   Assuming a minimal tax rate of 0.01% would still result in a volume decline by a third. Note that these calculations illustrate magnitudes at most, as data are available only from stock markets, not from foreign exchange markets.

5.3.4 Can any tax rate satisfy the guidance and the liquidity objective?

The competing objectives of guidance and liquidity that have governed the more recent Tobin tax discussion have led proponents to a clear reaction. Sorting the Tobin tax proposals by their date of issue reveals that the suggested rates have become lower and lower over time, with a new minimum suggested recently. A study by Spahn (2002) on behalf of the German Federal Ministry for Economic Cooperation and Development indicates a preference for a normal rate of 0.02% for an interbank transaction (0.01% on each participating bank per deal).

In the light of our above discussion, the Tobin tax proponents have adjusted their arguments first to the decline in transaction costs, and second to the fire attracted from the finance community regarding the liquidity concerns. There is no question that new proposals take market microstructure insights seriously. The problem, however, is that this move to satisfy one concern also clearly damages the original main concern. Reading the analyses carefully, there was never any hope that a Tobin tax could shelter currencies against major speculative attacks. The purpose was more modest – to limit the undesirable effects of "normal" speculative activities.

It is obvious and conceded by Spahn (2002) that low rates such as 0.02% will not impact speculative activity very much, if at all. This is accepted as the price for keeping the market liquid. What has not been considered so far, however, is that banks do not appear to be the right focus in any discussion of exchange rate speculation. It is asset managers who matter, and their horizon is clearly longer than that of FX dealers. Moreover, their horizon is definitely too long to be impacted by tax rates of below 0.1%. Microstructure research thus reveals the illusionary nature of those proposals featuring ever declining tax rates: even if the minimum rates might impact FX dealers' decisions – which is still questionable – the logic of the Tobin tax shows that minimum rates cannot influence the comparatively longer-term calculus of the asset managers.

Summing up, it would appear that there is no escape from the competing objectives discussed here, and that there is no support for hypothesis 4: a low rate does not curb speculation, and a high rate significantly reduces liquidity. The latter might even induce an unintended change in market structure. Frankel (1996, p.66) states that "such a change in market structure would be momentous". What are the possible policy alternatives under these circumstances?

5.4. Policy conclusions

Considering only the guidance and the liquidity objective, and leaving aside other the objectives of a Tobin tax, the original concept of a uniform proportional tax rate does not achieve its goals. First, microstructure research has only strengthened the case of Tobin tax opponents, by highlighting the economic benefit of risk allocation in foreign exchange markets and the consequent potential costs of a transaction tax. Second, the latest research has also undermined hopes that there could be any tax rate that is capable of satisfying the two competing objectives discussed here. The available evidence thus suggests that the Tobin tax concept was designed for a scenario of speculating banks and higher transaction costs that simply does not exist at present.

This finding leaves three alternative strategies open: first, one could follow the income-generating impetus of many proponents and simply accept that a minimum rate cannot guide foreign exchange markets; but why then tax FX transactions at all? Second, one may stick to Tobin's original concern and adopt guidance as the overarching priority, thus risking the unknown outcome of a massive liquidity reduction, and possibly even a tax-induced change in market structure; is this experiment worth it? It may be speculated that neither alternative is appropriate to what Tobin originally had in mind. Tobin (1996) may thus offer a third alternative, by shifting the basis of assessment away from transactions, and towards open positions. Whatever a serious analysis of this idea may reveal, the original Tobin tax concept is unconvincing in the light of recent microstructure research in foreign exchange.

References

Andersen, Torben G., Tim Bollerslev and Francis X. Diebold, 2003. Some like it smooth, and some like it rough: untangling continuous and jump components in measuring, modeling, and forecasting asset return volatility, working paper.

Andersen, Torben G., Tim Bollerslev and Nour Meddahi, 2003. Correcting the errors: volatility forecast evaluation using high-frequency data and realized volatilities, working paper.

Arestis, Philip and Malcolm Sawyer, 1997. How many cheers for the Tobin transactions tax?, *Cambridge Journal of Economics* 21, 753-768.

Bank for International Settlements, 1999. Triennial central bank survey, foreign exchange and derivatives market activity in 1998, Basel.

Bank for International Settlements, 2002. Triennial central bank survey, foreign exchange and derivatives market activity in 2001, Basel.

Bishop, Matthew, 2002. Crisis? What crisis?, in: Capitalism and its troubles: a survey of international finance, *The Economist* May 18th 2002, 1-28.

Bjønnes, Geir Høidal and Dagfinn Rime, 2001a. Customer trading and information in foreign exchange markets, working paper, Stockholm Institute for Financial Research.

Bjønnes, Geir Høidal and Dagfinn Rime, 2001b. FX trading … LIVE! Dealer behavior and trading systems in foreign exchange markets, working paper, Stockholm Institute for Financial Research.

Bjønnes, Geir Høidal and Dagfinn Rime, 2003. Dealer behavior and trading systems in foreign exchange markets, *Journal of Financial Economics*, forthcoming.

Bjønnes, Geir Høidal, Dagfinn Rime and Haakon O. Aa. Solheim, 2002. Volume and volatility in the FX-market: does it matter who you are?, CESIFO Working Paper 786.

Bjønnes, Geir Høidal, Dagfinn Rime and Haakon O. Aa. Solheim, 2003. Liquidity provision in the overnight foreign exchange market, working paper, Stockholm Institute for Financial Research.

Bollerslev, Tim and Ian Domowitz, 1993. Trading patterns and prices in the interbank foreign exchange market, *Journal of Finance* 48, 1421-1443.

Bollerslev, Tim and Michael Melvin, 1994. Bid-ask spreads and volatility in the foreign exchange market, *Journal of International Economics* 36, 355-372.

Braas, Albéric and Charles N. Bralver, 1990. An analysis of trading profits: how most trading rooms really make money, *Journal of Applied Corporate Finance* 2, 85-90.

Campbell, John Y. and Kenneth A. Froot, 1994. International experiences with securities transaction taxes, in: Jeffrey Frankel (ed.), The internationalization of equity markets, Chicago: University of Chicago Press, 277-308.

Cao, Henry H., Martin D.D. Evans and Richard K. Lyons, 2004. Inventory information, *Journal of Business*, forthcoming.

Carpenter, Andrew and Jianxin Wang, 2003. Sources of private information in FX trading, working paper, University of New South Wales, Australia.

Carter, David A. and Betty J. Simkins, 2002. Do markets react rationally? The effect of the September 11th tragedy on airline stock returns, working paper OK 74078-4011, Oklahoma State University, Stillwater.

Cheung, Yin-Wong and Menzie D. Chinn, 2001. Currency traders and exchange rate dynamics: a survey of the US market, *Journal of International Money and Finance* 20, 439-471.

Cheung, Yin-Wong, Menzie D. Chinn and Ian W. Marsh, 2000. How do UK-based foreign exchange dealers think their market operates?, NBER Working Paper 7524.

Chordia, Tarun, Richard Roll and Avanidhar Subrahmanyam, 2001. Market liquidity and trading activity, *Journal of Finance* 56, 501-530.

Chordia, Tarun, Richard Roll and Avanidhar Subrahmanyam, 2002. Order imbalance, liquidity, and market returns, *Journal of Financial Economics* 65, 111-130.

Chow, Gregory C., 1960. Tests of equality between sets of coefficients in two linear regressions, *Econometrica* 28, 591-605.

Chu, Jennifer, and Carol Osler, 2004. Microstructural consequences of imperfect rationality: the head-and-shoulders pattern in currency markets, Mimeo, Brandeis International Business School.

Clark, Peter K., 1973. A subordinated stochastic process model with finite variance for speculative prices, *Econometrica* 41, 135-155.

Copeland, Thomas E., 1976. A model of asset trading under the assumption of sequential information arrival, *Journal of Finance* 31, 1149-1168.

Copeland, Thomas E. and Dan Galai, 1983. Information effects on the bid-ask spread, *Journal of Finance* 31, 1457-1469.

Cornell, Bradford, 1978. Determinants of the bid-ask spread on forward foreign exchange contracts under floating exchange rates, *Journal of International Business Studies* 9, 33-41.

Covrig, Vicentiu and Michael Melvin, 2002. Asymmetric information and price discovery in the FX market: does Tokyo know more about the Yen?, *Journal of Empirical Finance* 9, 271-285.

Danielson, Jon and Richard Payne, 2001. Measuring and explaining liquidity on an electronic limit order book: evidence from Reuters D2000-2, working paper.

Danielsson, Jon and Richard Payne, 2002. Real trading patterns and prices in spot foreign exchange markets, *Journal of International Money and Finance* 21, 203-222.

Dominguez, Kathryn M.E., 2003. The market microstructure of central bank intervention, *Journal of International Economics* 59, 25-45.

Easley, David and Maureen O'Hara, 1987. Price trade size and information in securities markets, *Journal of Financial Economics* 19, 69-90.

Easley, David, Soeren Hvidkjaer and Maureen O'Hara, 2002. Is information risk a determinant of asset prices?, *Journal of Finance* 57, 2185-2221.

Eichengreen, Barry, 1996. The Tobin tax: What have we learned?, in: ul Haq et al. (eds.), 1996, 273-287.

Eichengreen, Barry, James Tobin and Charles Wyplosz, 1995. Two cases for throwing sand in the wheels of international finance, *Economic Journal* 105, 162-172.

Evans, Martin D.D., 2002. FX trading and exchange rate dynamics, *Journal of Finance* 57, 2405-2447.

Evans, Martin D.D. and Richard K. Lyons, 2002. Order flow and exchange rate dynamics, *Journal of Political Economy* 110, 170-180.

Evans, Martin D.D. and Richard K. Lyons, 2003. How is macro news transmitted to exchange rates, NBER Working Paper 9433.

Fan, Mintao and Richard K. Lyons, 2003. Customer trades and extreme events in foreign exchange, in: Paul Mizen (ed.), Monetary history, exchange rates and financial markets: essays in honour of Charles Goodhart, Northampton: Edward Elgar, 160-179.

Faust, Jon, John H. Rogers and Jonathan H. Wright, 2003. Exchange rate forecasting: the errors we've really made, *Journal of International Economics* 60, 35-59.

Fieleke, Norman S., 1981. Foreign-currency positioning by U.S. firms: some new evidence, *Review of Economics and Statistics* 63, 35-42.

Flood, Mark D., 1994. Market structure and inefficiency in the foreign exchange market, *Journal of International Money and Finance* 13, 131-158.

Flood, Robert P. and Mark P. Taylor, 1996. Exchange rate economics: what's wrong with the conventional macro approach?, in: Frankel, Jeffrey A., Giampaolo Galli, and Alberto Giovannini (eds.), The microstructure of foreign exchange markets, University of Chicago Press, Chicago 1996, 261-294.

Frankel, Jeffrey A., 1996. How well do markets work: might a Tobin tax help?, in: ul Haq et al. (eds.), 1996, 41-81.

Frankel, Jeffrey A. and Andrew Rose, 1995. Empirical research on nominal exchange rates, in: Gene Grossmann and Kenneth Rogoff (eds.), Handbook of International Economics, Vol.III, Amsterdam et al.: North-Holland, 1689-1729.

Frankel, Jeffrey A. and Shang-Jin Wei, 1991. Are option-implied forecasts of exchange rate volatility excessively variable?, NBER Working Paper 3910.

Froot, Kenneth A. and Takatoshi Ito, 1989. On the consistency of short-run and long-run exchange rate expectations, Journal of International Money and Finance 8, 487-510.

Froot, Kenneth A. and Tarun Ramadorai, 2002. Currency returns, institutional investor flows, and exchange rate fundamentals, NBER Working Paper 9080.

Galati, Gabriele, 2003. Trading volume, volatility and spreads in foreign exchange markets: evidence from emerging market countries, working paper.

Galati, Gabriele, William Melick and Marian Micu, 2003. Foreign exchange market intervention and expectations: an empirical study of the yen/dollar exchange rate, BIS Working Paper.

Gammill, James F., 1989. The organization of financial markets: competitive versus cooperative market mechanisms. Harvard University Mimeo.

Gehrig, Thomas and Lukas Menkhoff, 2004. The use of flow analysis in foreign exchange: exploratory evidence, Journal of International Money and Finance 23, 573-594.

Glosten, L., and Paul Milgrom, 1985. Bid, ask, and transaction prices in a specialist market with heterogeneously informed agents, Journal of Financial Economics 14, 71-100.

Goodhart, Charles A.E., 1988. The foreign exchange market: a random walk with a dragging anchor, Economica 55, 437-460.

Goodhart, Charles and Lorenzo Figliuoli, 1991. Every minute counts in financial markets, Journal of International Money and Finance 10, 23-52.

Goodhart, Charles, Ryan Love, Richard Payne and Dagfinn Rime, 2002. Analysis of spread in the Dollar/Euro and Deutsche-Mark/Dollar foreign exchange markets, Economic Policy 17:35, 536-552.

Goodhart, Charles, Takatoshi Ito and Richard Payne, 1996. One day in June 1993: a study of the working of the Reuters 2000-2 electronic foreign exchange trading system, in: Frankel, Jeffrey A., Giampaolo Galli, and Alberto Giovannini (eds.), The microstructure of foreign exchange markets, University of Chicago Press, Chicago 1996, 107-179.

Habermeier, Karl and Andrei A. Kirilenko, 2002. Securities transaction taxes and financial markets. Paper presented at the Third Annual IMF Research Conference, November.

Harris, Lawrence, 1986. Cross-security tests of the mixture of distributions hypothesis, Journal of Financial and Quantitative Analysis 21, 39-46.

Hartmann, Philipp, 1999. Trading volumes and transaction costs in the foreign exchange market, Journal of Banking and Finance 23, 801-824.

Hasbrouck, Joel, 1991. Measuring the information content of stock trades, *Journal of Finance* 46, 178-208.

Hasbrouck, Joel and Duane J. Seppi, 2001. Common factors in prices, order flows, and liquidity, *Journal of Financial Economics* 59, 383-411.

Hau, Harald, 2002. The role of transaction costs for financial volatility: Evidence from the Paris bourse, working paper, INSEAD.

Hau, Harald, William P. Killeen and Michael J. Moore, 2000. The euro as an international currency: explaining puzzling first evidence, CEPR discussion paper 2510.

Hau, Harald, William P. Killeen and Michael J. Moore, 2002. How has the Euro changed the foreign exchange market?, *Economic Policy* 34, 149-191.

Ho, T. and Hans R. Stoll, 1981. Optimal dealer pricing under transactions and return uncertainty, *Journal of Financial Economics* 9, 47-73.

Hon, Mark T., Jack Strauss and Soo-Keong Yong, 2004. Contagion in financial markets after September 11th: myth or reality?, *Journal of Financial Research* 27, 95-114.

Huang, Roger D. and Hans R. Stoll, 1997. The components of the bid-ask spread: a general approach, *Review of Financial Studies* 10, 995-1034.

Ito, Takatoshi, Richard K. Lyons and Michael Melvin, 1998. Is there private information in the FX market? The Tokyo experiment, *Journal of Finance* 53, 1111-1130.

Jorion, Philippe, 1996. Risk and turnover in the foreign exchange market, in: Frankel, Jeffrey A., Giampaolo Galli, and Alberto Giovannini (eds.), The microstructure of foreign exchange markets, University of Chicago Press, Chicago 1996, 19-36.

Karpoff, Jonathan, 1987. The relation between price changes and trading volume: a survey, *Journal of Financial and Quantitative Analysis* 22, 109-126.

Keynes, John Maynard, 1936. The general theory on employment, interest, and money, New York, London: HBJ Book (reprint).

Kilian, Lutz and Mark P. Taylor, 2003. Why is it so difficult to beat the random walk forecast of exchange rates?, *Journal of International Economics* 60, 85-107.

Killeen, William P., Richard K. Lyons and Michael J. Moore, 2001. Fixed versus floating: lessons from EMS order flow, NBER Working Paper 8491.

Koopman, Siem Jan, Borus Jungbacken and Eugenie Hol, 2004. Forecasting daily variability of the S&P stock index using historical, realized and implied volatility measurements, Tinbergen Institute Discussion Paper TI 2004-016/4.

Kyle, Albert S., 1985. Continuous auctions and insider trading, *Econometrica* 53, 1315-1335.

Leach, J. Chris and Ananth N. Madhavan, 1992, Intertemporal price discovery by market makers: Active versus passive learning, *Journal of Financial Intermediation* 2, 207-235.

Leach, J. Chris and Ananth N. Madhavan, 1993. Price experimentation and security market structure, *Review of Financial Studies* 6, 375-404.

Lui, Yu-Hon and David Mole, 1998. The use of fundamental and technical analysis by foreign exchange dealers: Hong Kong evidence, *Journal of International Money and Finance* 17, 535-545.

Lyons, Richard K., 1995. Tests of microstructural hypotheses in the foreign exchange market, *Journal of Financial Economics* 39, 321-351.

Lyons, Richard K., 1996. Foreign exchange volume: sound and fury signifying nothing?, in: Frankel, Jeffrey A., Giampaolo Galli, and Alberto Giovannini (eds.), The microstructure of foreign exchange markets, University of Chicago Press, Chicago 1996, 183-201.

Lyons, Richard K., 1997. A simultaneous trade model of the foreign exchange hot potato, *Journal of International Economics* 42, 275-298.

Lyons, Richard K., 1998. Profits and position control: a week of FX dealing, *Journal of International Money and Finance* 17, 97-115.

Lyons, Richard K., 2001a. The microstructure approach to exchange rates. Cambridge: MIT Press.

Lyons, Richard K., 2001b. New perspective on FX markets: order-flow analysis, *International Finance* 4, 303-320.

MacDonald, Ronald, 2000. Expectations formation and risk in three financial markets: surveying what the surveys say, *Journal of Economic Surveys* 14: 69-100.

Madhavan, Ananth, 2000. Market microstructure: a survey, *Journal of Financial Markets* 3, 205-258.

Madhavan, Ananth and Seymour Smidt, 1991. A Bayesian model of intraday specialist pricing, *Journal of Financial Economics* 30, 99-134.

Meese, Richard and Kenneth Rogoff, 1983. Empirical exchange rate models of the seventies: do they fit out of sample?, *Journal of International Economics* 14, 3-24.

Melvin, Michael and Xixi Yin, 2000. Public information arrival, exchange rate volatility, and quote frequency, *Economic Journal* 110, 644-661.

Mende, Alexander, 2002. Hot potato trading, *Wirtschaftswissenschaftliches Studium* 31, 223-227.

Mende, Alexander and Lukas Menkhoff, 2003a. Tobin tax effects seen from the foreign exchange market's microstructure, *International Finance* 6, 227-247.

Mende, Alexander and Lukas Menkhoff, 2003b. Different counterparties, different foreign exchange trading? The perspective of a median bank, discussion paper, University of Hannover.

Mende, Alexander and Lukas Menkhoff, 2004. Profit sources in FX trading, working paper.

Mende, Alexander, Lukas Menkhoff and Carol Osler, 2004. Strategic dealing in currency markets, working paper.

Menkhoff, Lukas, 1997. Examining the use of technical currency analysis, *International Journal of Finance and Economics* 2, 307-318.

Menkhoff, Lukas, 2001. Short-term horizons in foreign exchange? Survey evidence from dealers and fund managers, *Kyklos* 54, 27-47.

Neely, Christopher and Lucio Sarno, 2002. How well do monetary fundamentals forecast exchange rates?, Federal Reserve Bank of St. Louis Review 84, 51-74.

Osler, Carol L., 1998. Short-term speculators and the puzzling behavior of exchange rates, *Journal of International Economics* 45, 37-57.

Osler, Carol L., 2002. Stop-loss orders and price cascades in currency markets, Federal Reserve Bank of New York Staff Paper No. 150.

Osler, Carol L., 2003. Currency orders and exchange-rate dynamics: an explanation for the predictive success of technical analysis, *Journal of Finance* 58: 1791-1819.

Payne, Richard, 2003. Informed trade in spot foreign exchange markets: an empirical investigation, *Journal of International Economics* 61, 307-329.

Payne, Richard and Paolo Vitale, 2003. A transaction level study of the effects of central bank intervention on exchange rates, *Journal of International Economics* 61, 331-352.

Peiers, Bettina, 1997. Informed traders, intervention and price leadership: a deeper view of the microstructure of the foreign exchange market, *Journal of Finance* 52, 1589-1614.

Petersen, Mark A, and Erik Sirri, 2003. Order preferencing and market quality on U.S. equity exchanges, *Review of Financial Studies* 16: 385-415.

Poon, Ser-Huang, Bevan Blair and Stephen Taylor, 2001. Forecasting S&P 100 volatility: using high frequency data and implied volatility, *Journal of Econometrics* 105, 5-26.

Reisen, Helmut, 2002. Tobin tax: could it work?, *OECD Observer* No. 231/232, March.

Rime, Dagfinn, 2000. U.S. exchange rates and currency flows, working paper, Stockholm Institute for Financial Research.

Rime, Dagfinn, 2003. New electronic trading systems in foreign exchange markets, in: Jones, Derek C. (ed.), New Economy Handbook, Academic Press 2003.

Rogoff, Kenneth, 1996. The purchasing power parity puzzle, *Journal of Economic Literature* 34, 647-668.

Rogoff, Kenneth, 2002. Dornbusch's overshooting model after twenty-five years. IMF Mundell-Fleming Lecture, IMF Working Paper WP/02/39.

Romeu, Rafael, 2003. An intraday pricing model of foreign exchange markets, IMF Working Paper WP/03/115.

Sarno, Lucio and Mark P. Taylor, 2001. The microstructure of the foreign-exchange market: a selective survey of the literature, *Princeton Studies in International Economics* No. 89, Princeton University.

Sarno, Lucio and Mark P. Taylor, 2002. The economics of exchange rates. Cambridge et al: Cambridge University Press

Sarr, Abdourahmana and Tonny Lybek, 2002. Measuring liquidity in financial markets, IMF Working Paper WP/02/232.

Shleifer, Andrei, 1986. Do demand curves for stocks slope down?, *Journal of Finance* 41, 579-590.

Spahn, Paul Bernd, 2002. On the feasibility of a tax on foreign exchange transactions, report to the Federal Ministry for Economic Cooperation and Development, Bonn.

Sweeney, Richard J., 1997. Do central banks lose on foreign-exchange intervention? A review article, *Journal of Banking and Finance* 21, 1667-1684.

Tauchen, George E. and Mark Pitts, 1983. The price variability-volume relationship on speculative markets, *Econometrica* 51, 485-505.

Taylor, Mark P., 1995. Exchange rate economics, *Journal of Economic Literature* 33, 13-47.

Taylor, Mark P., 2003. Purchasing power parity, *Review of International Economics* 11, 436-452.

Taylor, Mark P. and Helen Allen, 1992. The use of technical analysis in the foreign exchange market, *Journal of International Money and Finance* 11, 304-314.

Tobin, James, 1978. A proposal for international monetary reform, *Eastern Economic Journal* 4, 153-159.

Tobin, James, 1984. On the efficiency of the financial system, *Lloyds Bank Review* No.153, 1-15.

Tobin, James, 1996. Prologue, in: ul-Haq et al. (eds.), 1996, ix-xviii.

Ul Haq, Mahbub, Inge Kaul and Isabelle Grunberg (eds.),1996. The Tobin tax: coping with financial volatility, Oxford et al.: Oxford University Press.

Vitale, Paolo, 1999. Sterilized central bank intervention in the foreign exchange market, *Journal of International Economics* 49, 245-267.

Wahl, Peter and Peter Waldow, 2001. Currency transaction tax – a concept with a future. WEED (world economy, ecology & development) working paper, Bonn.

Wang, George H.K. and Jot Yau, 2000. Trading volume, bid-ask spread, and price volatility in future markets, *The Journal of Futures Markets* 20, 943-970.

Wei, Shang-Jin, 1994. Anticipations of foreign exchange volatility and bid-ask spreads, NBER Working Paper 4737.

Wei, Shang-Jin and Junshik Kim, 1997. The big players in the foreign exchange market: do they trade on information or noise?, NBER Working Paper 6256.

Yao, Jian M., 1998a. Market making in the interbank foreign exchange market. Working paper S-98-3, Stern School of Business, New York University.

Yao, Jian M., 1998b. Spread components and dealer profits in the interbank foreign exchange market. Working paper S-98-4, Stern School of Business, New York University.

Studien zu Internationalen Wirtschaftsbeziehungen

Herausgegeben von Prof. Dr. Michael Frenkel

Band 1   Christiane Nickel: Insider und Outsider bei der Osterweiterung der Europäischen Währungsunion. 2002.

Band 2   Georg Stadtmann: Noise-Trader auf Devisenmärkten. Viel Lärm um Nichts? 2002.

Band 3   Wolf-Heimo Grieben: Trade and Technology as Competing Explanations for Rising Inequality. An Endogenous Growth Perspective. 2003.

Band 4   Alexander Mende: Order Flow Analyses and Foreign Exchange Dealing. 2005.

www.peterlang.de